The Phoenix in the Sky
Tales of Wonder and Wisdom from World Religions

Indira Ananthakrishnan has been writing and telling stories for many years. She has written several award-winning short stories, historical tales, biographical sketches, plays and picture books. She has a special interest in reading and interpreting the scriptures and making them creatively appealing for young readers.

THE PHOENIX IN THE SKY

Tales of Wonder and Wisdom from World Religions

Indira Ananthakrishnan

Illustrations by Sahitya Rani

hachette INDIA

First published in 2020 by Hachette India
(Registered name: Hachette Book Publishing India Pvt. Ltd)
An Hachette UK company
www.hachetteindia.com

SRD

ISBN 978-93-89253-61-0

Hachette Book Publishing India Pvt. Ltd
4th & 5th Floors, Corporate Centre
Plot No. 94, Sector 44, Gurugram – 122003, India

Typeset in Tiempo
by Manmohan Kumar, Delhi

Printed and bound in India
by Manipal Technologies Limited, Manipal

MIX
Paper from responsible sources
FSC™ C043100

CONTENTS

What we know about most of the religious leaders and teachers described in the book is through stories people have narrated down generations or through oral histories. These stories give clues to events, but may not be exact histories, as they are influenced by the storytellers' own perceptions and background. The author of this book has tried to select the most significant of these events from these histories about the figures, and those most relevant to their teachings and to the readers.

THE BANQUET

A long time ago, in the thirteenth century, there lived a wise scholar in Turkey named Naseerudin Hodja. Hodja means 'teacher'. Naseerudin had an unusual method of teaching people. He told them anecdotes that they could relate to easily. At the same time, the incidents he spoke about taught them something about the ways of life. Some people admired him for his wit and sense of humour, while others scorned him for his unconventional ways. But Naseerudin Hodja did not mind being laughed at as long as his jesting was of use to somebody.

Once, a royal banquet was arranged for all the scholars in the kingdom. Everyone came dressed in their best clothes. Naseerudin Hodja came too, but reluctantly. Not being particularly excited about the event, he wore the plainest clothes he had.

One by one, all the scholars entered the banquet hall. Hodja, though, was stopped at the entrance.

'Why are you stopping me from entering? I have been invited to the banquet,' Naseerudin said.

'Your clothes,' replied the gatekeeper.

Naseerudin looked at himself for a moment and said, 'And pray, what is wrong with my clothes? They are absolutely clean and neat.'

Seeing the commotion, the master of ceremonies went up to Naseerudin and hissed, 'You are disrespecting the hosts. Don't you know that a proper dress code must be maintained for such events?'

Without a word, Naseerudin turned around and walked away.

After some time, he was back, dressed in shiny, silken garments with large pockets, a glittering turban and golden slippers. He was now welcomed warmly. He went in, bowed deeply, took his allotted seat and looked around.

Prayers were chanted and the food was served. Wonderful aromas filled the hall as platters piled high with rich and exotic foods kept appearing. The guests slurped and chewed noisily and swallowed big mouthfuls.

All except Naseerudin.

He did nothing of the sort. Not one morsel of food went into his mouth. Instead, he took handfuls of each dish and stuffed his large pockets with it, humming

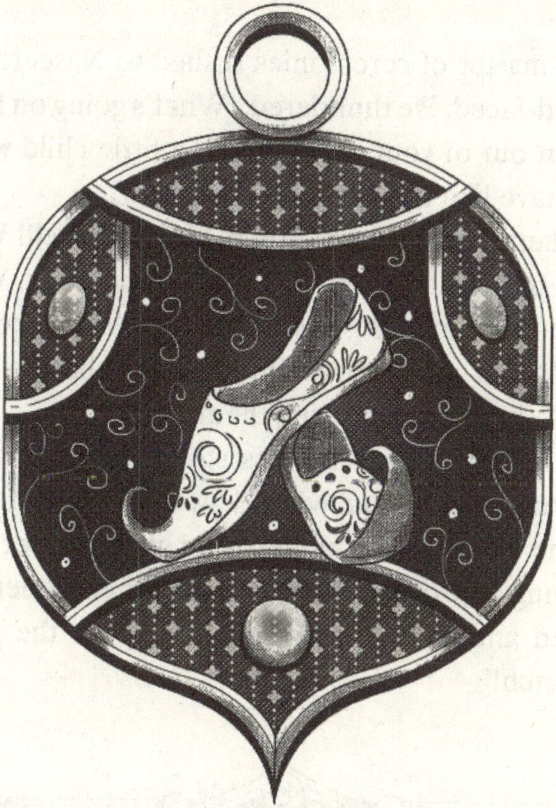

softly,

'Eat, my dear coat, eat,
There are savouries and sweets,
Indeed a great treat!
Trippa...tee...tee!'

People stopped eating. Servers stopped serving. A hush fell in the hall as everyone looked at Naseerudin in utter horror.

The master of ceremonies rushed to Naseerudin's side, red-faced. He thundered, 'What's going on here? Are you out of your mind? Even a little child would not behave like this at a royal banquet.'

Naseerudin was unperturbed. He said, 'Well! When I came in ordinary clothes, I was turned away. When I came back in this silken attire, I was welcomed. Doesn't that mean the banquet is for these clothes and not the person wearing them?'

The master of ceremonies stood dumfounded as Naseerudin got up and walked away.

Some guests, who understood what Naseerudin was trying to prove, nodded to each other. Others just frowned and said, 'Naseerudin has spoilt the party, the wretch!'

Naseerudin Hodja was famous in his home country of Turkey, and tales of his sharp wit and humour are known throughout the world.

THE LITTLE SQUIRREL ON THE SEASHORE

Rama, the prince of Ayodhya, sat under a lone tree on the seashore with a heavy heart. The vast Indian Ocean lay between him and the kingdom of Lanka, where Sita, his dear wife, was being held captive.

The ocean had to be crossed. The army of monkeys, led by their king, Sugriva, and his minister Hanuman, was going to build a bridge over it, but it was not an easy task.

On the tree lived a little squirrel and her mother. The young squirrel ran up and down the tree, excited at the sight of the monkeys. When she saw Rama, she stood for a moment staring at him with unblinking eyes. Rama smiled at her. The squirrel screeched with happiness and quickly scampered away.

When the squirrel learnt why the monkeys were building the bridge, she wanted to help them.

'But be careful. The monkeys could easily trample you,' her mother said, worried.

The little squirrel scurried down the tree, eager to get started. She saw the monkeys carrying big boulders and ruddy rocks that would form the base of the bridge.

She looked around here and there, but of course she was too tiny to carry any of the rocks. The only things she could lift were the pebbles! So she chose a round pebble as big as the nuts she was used to carrying and put it in her mouth. The pebble felt heavy, but she bravely ran with it to the seashore and dropped it amongst the stones the monkeys were arranging.

The next moment she heard loud laughter.

'Little squirrel, do you think your pebble is going to be of any use to us? Just look at your size – you could spend a lifetime carrying pebbles and it will still be completely useless!' the monkeys jeered.

The squirrel tried hard not to burst into tears in front of them and quickly scuttled away. She said to her mother sadly, 'Amma! I am *too* small. I can't help Rama.'

'If you really want to do something, you can and you will,' her mother said firmly.

The little squirrel ran back down and watched the monkeys at work. 'What can I do?' she thought long and hard.

Suddenly, she saw a monkey carrying a huge rock coming close to her. Just as she leapt aside to avoid being trampled, she noticed that his wet feet were covered with sand.

Her eyes sparkled.

'I know what I can do!' she squeaked. She did not waste another moment.

She dashed to the water and jumped in with a splash. Rama watched her quizzically.

Then he saw her run back to the sandy shore and roll herself in the dry sand. She soon looked like a little sand ball!

Sand-ball Squirrel now made a beeline for the bridge and shook herself, letting all the sand from her body fall into the gap between the stones.

Then she went back into the water and the whole cycle of wetting, rolling-in-the-sand and bristling-on-the-bridge started again. The little squirrel did this again and again and again till sundown!

Darkness fell. The monkeys finished their work. The bridge was done.

Hanuman and Sugriva had a final look at it. The bridge stood firm, the sand binding the stones together. *But where had the sand come from?* everyone wondered.

No one knew except Rama.

He picked up the little squirrel, stroked her back gently with three of his fingers and whispered, 'Thank you.' He then held her up, raised his voice and said, 'I am grateful to everyone, from the biggest of you to the smallest one here in my hand, for building this bridge.'

The tiny squirrel was too happy to even squeak!

This incident is referred to in Kamban's Ramayana (a version of the holy text written by the poet Kamban in Tamil). It is said that the three stripes on a squirrel's back are the marks made by Rama's fingers when he stroked the little creature that day at the seashore.

THE GOOD SAMARITAN

The Samaritans were a small group of people who lived in the central region of ancient Israel. The Jews considered the religious beliefs of the Samaritans strange and unconventional, and so they did not get along.

Jesus was really unhappy about the way the Jews behaved towards the Samaritans. He wanted the two communities to live in harmony. But how could he make them understand, he wondered. A parable* would help, he finally decided.

Jesus was sitting on the shores of the Sea of Galilee, thinking about this, when a devout Jew approached him. Jesus looked up at him questioningly.

The Jew asked, 'What do I need to do to be eternally happy?'

'You seem to have already given it some thought. Tell me, what do you know about eternal happiness?' Jesus asked instead.

*A simple story used to teach a moral lesson

The man promptly replied, 'Loving God with all my heart and loving my neighbour. That's what I have been taught I must do for eternal happiness.'

'Good. Go home and do just that,' said Jesus.

'But,' the man persisted, 'I don't understand who my neighbour is. Is he the one living next door or the one living opposite me, or the one in the next street or…' His voice trailed off doubtfully.

Jesus's parable took shape immediately. He stood up and spread out his arms. The people around him knew he was going to address them. They gathered in front of him and looked up at him expectantly.

Jesus spoke in a loud and resonating voice.

'One evening, a well-dressed elderly Jew was walking from Jerusalem to Jericho. The sun had set. The road was gradually getting enveloped in darkness. The man hastened his steps. He had to reach his destination before dark. In the surrounding silence, he suddenly heard footsteps behind him. They were steadily getting closer. The man took the name of the lord, clutched his purse and walked faster. But soon, the footsteps were right next to him. A pair of hands grabbed his purse. They then stripped him of his clothes. When he tried to protect himself, he was beaten up. The more he struggled, the more he was beaten. They left him half-dead and gasping for breath.

'No one came down that road for a while. The man moaned and groaned. At last, a Jewish priest walked by, a rosary in his right hand. In the fading light, his eyes fell on the wounded man lying on the roadside.

'"Good Lord," he exclaimed and bent down for a better look. He held his breath. "This poor man needs help. But I can't do much. I can't stand the sight of blood. I hope someone else comes along soon," he murmured. Without tarrying another moment, he crossed the road and walked away.

'A short while later, a Levite* came along. He too stopped and looked at the wounded man. "Poor fellow! He's at death's door. I wish I could help him. But I have to be going. I have evening duty at the temple. I'll pray for him." So saying, the Levite hurried away.

'The wounded man could hardly breathe now. Even his groaning had stopped. Now a third man, a young Samaritan, came down the road riding on his donkey. When he saw the dying man, he stopped and jumped off his donkey. The moonlight revealed the man's pathetic condition. Instantly, the Samaritan fell on his knees, picked the man up and gently laid him on his donkey's back. The man groaned feebly.

'"Don't worry. You'll be all right," the Samaritan said softly and directed the donkey to the nearest inn.

*A member of the Levi tribe. The Levites performed religious duties at Jewish temples.

There, with the innkeeper's help, he washed and dressed the man's wounds. He then opened his purse and gave the innkeeper the two silver coins that were in it.

'"Here, take this," he told the innkeeper. "Some warm milk and a bed for this poor man, please. If you need more money to look after him, I'll give it to you in the morning."

'The Samaritan then went his way.' Jesus stopped here, and turned to the Jew who'd come to him and said, 'Now tell me, who is the wounded man's neighbour?'

'The good Samaritan who treated him kindly,' came the reply.

The crowd rose to leave. Jesus concluded, 'We are one another's neighbours, all of us. Let's learn to be kind and compassionate, like the good Samaritan.'

This parable inspired the phrase 'good Samaritan', which is widely used in modern times. A good Samaritan is a person who helps someone in need because they are considerate, not because they're looking for any type of reward – just like the Samaritan in Jesus's tale.

MOTHER TERESA

Mother Teresa believed in the power of love and acceptance. Whatever she thought, spoke or did was associated with love.

By blood, Mother Teresa was an Albanian named Anjezë at birth. By faith, she was a Catholic nun, Sister Teresa, who later came to be known as Mother Teresa. By citizenship, she was Indian. But she believed that she belonged to the world.

In the early twentieth century, girls were not permitted to attend school. So Anjezë was homeschooled. Her mother brought her up lovingly, and had a big influence on Anjezë's personality and how she viewed the world. The head priest of the youth group at their local church found her eager to learn other subjects besides religion. He taught her science, medicine and art.

Anjezë's calling, which was devotion to God and service to the people, began to echo in her heart from the age of 12. At 18, she joined a convent of Irish nuns called the Sisters of Loreto. She was a favourite with the other nuns. Since she was short and slim, they used to say, 'Sister Teresa hides her large heart in a diminutive figure!'

Loreto Convent sent her to India for service. She enjoyed teaching at their school in Kolkata, then called Calcutta. Her students loved and respected her greatly.

Not very long afterwards came Mother Teresa's second calling, when she saw the sadness among the poorer classes of society. She felt an intense urge to serve the poor and the needy. Her determination, courage, capacity for hard work and talent for organization gave rise to the Missionaries of Charity, a religious order to help the destitute. She gave up her teaching career and worked at the mission. Many volunteers, especially those who were her students, offered to join her in her good work. She took intensive medical training in order to nurse the sick. She would start each day with a prayer and then visit poor families who needed her help, care for the sick lying uncared for on the roads and nurse those dying of hunger and tuberculosis.

The value of the work of the mission grew immensely because it was done with love and compassion. Financial support poured in. The mission expanded to aid lepers who were shunned by society. More missions were established in other underdeveloped countries. The poorest of the poor and the forsaken were able to live with dignity, and when they died, they were given a proper burial. Mother Teresa was hailed as the mother of the poor. She received the Nobel Peace Prize for her work in 1979.

Mother Teresa died at the age of 87. She was named a saint nearly two decades after her death by the Roman Catholic Church.

She often said:

'It is not how much we do, but how much love we put in doing. It is not how much we give, but how much love we put in giving.'

A CUP OF NECTAR

Yo-Huan sat at the Zen master's feet and listened attentively to his teachings.

One day, the master said, 'You may now go and practise all that you have learnt. Remember to come back on this same day next year and tell me about what you have done.'

After one year, on the same day, Yo-Huan set off to meet the master. Halfway down the path a sparrow with a broken wing, fighting for life, fell at his feet. If he stopped to help the bird, he would be late. He hesitated for just a moment before choosing to help the bird. Falling on his knees, he picked up the sparrow very gently and retraced his path till he came to a healer.

Yo-Huan waited till the healer mended its wing. In a short while, the sparrow shook itself and tried to take off. The healer smiled and said, 'Now you may go. The little one will soon fly.'

Yo-Huan heaved a sigh of relief, thanked the healer and left. It was almost evening when he reached his master's side. Yo-Huan could see he was displeased. He humbly sat at his master's feet and told him about what had happened on the way. The master's face softened into a smile. He patted Yo-Huan on the back and said, 'Well done! Now you are truly worthy of being a Zen master.'

Yo-Huan left his master's abode and started teaching. His teachings drew many disciples to him.

The number of people who came to him grew to such an extent that Yo-Huan had to build a monastery for his disciples. As more joined him, he divided them into two groups, seniors and juniors.

But the juniors were not happy with this division and constantly complained about it.

One day, Yo-Huan sent the seniors out into the world, just as his master had sent him, to practise what they had been taught.

The juniors muttered to each other, 'Why didn't he send us too?'

When the seniors came back, Yo-Huan arranged a graduation ceremony for them.

'Our master clearly prefers our seniors. They get special treatment all the time!' the juniors whispered amongst themselves.

When the ceremony was over, Yo-Huan said to the seniors, 'Now you will all taste the Zen nectar.'

Everybody was eager to taste the nectar. The juniors sat at a table to the right of the master and the seniors sat to his left.

'He's dividing us even now!' the juniors mumbled.

The nectar was served in small cups, first to the juniors, who were glad that they were going to get to taste it before the seniors. But just as they were about to take a sip, the master said, 'The nectar will purify you only if you drink it without bending your elbows. So please do not bend your elbows while drinking.'

When the disciples raised the cups to their lips they found that their elbows were bent. So they straightened their elbows, but then the cups would not reach their mouths, no matter what they did. The nectar streamed into some people's ears. Some of them ended up pouring it over their heads. And the nectar from the rest of the cups just sloshed all over the floor. Not one of them could taste even a drop of the nectar. The master and the seniors watched in silence, while the disappointed juniors cleaned up without a word.

The nectar was then served to the seniors. They arranged themselves in two rows facing one another. Without bending their elbows, each raised their cup to the lips of the person sitting across them. Not a

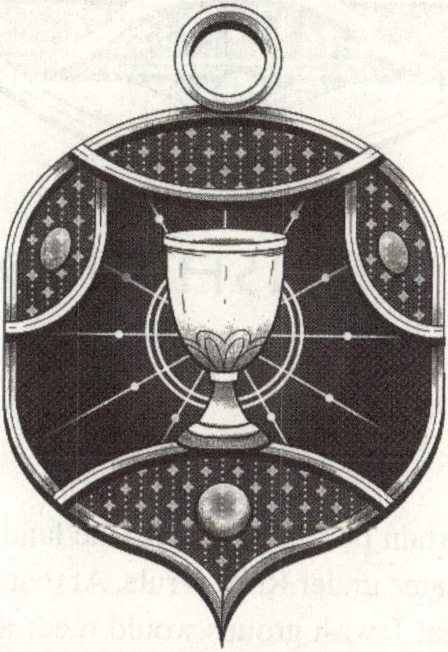

drop of nectar was spilled or wasted, and everyone had a taste of it.

The juniors understood why they were not yet ready to be senior disciples of their master.

Zen stories were originally passed on by word of mouth amongst the followers of Mahayana Buddhism. Now they have become universally popular because the values they teach are for all times and can be applied to everyday life.

THE FISH AND THE FOX

For a certain period in history, the land of ancient Israel came under Roman rule. At that time, every evening, local Jewish groups would meet and eagerly listen to their rabbis read from the Torah, their holy scroll. It helped them live a life of joy and courage.

Even though the Jews were a minority when the Romans were in power, the authorities of the land eyed them with distrust. They feared that the Jews would find too much strength by reading the Torah. 'They'll become brave and overpower us sooner or later,' they thought.

So they made reading the Torah punishable by law. The Jews were aghast. It pained them to put away their scrolls and stop congregating to read the scriptures. They were lost without the ideas in the Torah to guide them. They felt their lives were not worth living anymore.

This disturbed one of the rabbis greatly, but he was not discouraged. He continued to recite from the Torah and asked the community to join him. The people were thunderstruck. They cried, 'But defying the orders of the authorities will put us in trouble.'

The rabbi chuckled. He led his people to a lake full of clear water and asked, 'What do you see in the lake?'

Everyone crouched to have a look and said, 'We see many kinds of fish swimming hither and thither with not a moment's rest.'

'Why do you think they are doing that?' asked the rabbi.

'They're looking for food,' said some.

'That's their nature,' some others said.

There was a short pause, and then a bright, young girl got up and said, 'Maybe they are scared.'

'Why do you think so?' queried the rabbi.

'They dread the fisherman's net, I think,' replied the girl.

'That's exactly what the fish told the hungry fox,' said the rabbi. He continued, 'One day, a fox came to the lakeside, hoping to get some fish for his next meal. But he had to entice them out of the water, so he came up with a plan. He asked them why they were swimming so frantically, knowing that they were scared of getting trapped in a fisherman's net. When they told him the reason, the cunning fox asked the fish to come ashore so that they could be safe with him, instead of getting caught in the net. But the fish refused. They knew that if they went ashore, they would not be able to live for more than a few seconds without water. On the other hand, in the lake they could breathe and live. And maybe there was a chance they would escape the fisherman's net after all. The disappointed fox went away.'

The listeners looked at the rabbi, baffled. All of them, except the girl, wondered what the meaning of the story was. She alone smiled and thanked the rabbi. She then told the others what she had understood from the story. Everyone was happy. They went with the rabbi and settled down to read the Torah.

What did the girl say?

'Like the fish who feared the fisherman, we too fear the authorities. But the fish did not abandon the lake, their only means of survival. Therefore, we too should not abandon our study of the Torah. If we do, we may lose all hope in life.'

Why is reading the Torah so important in Judaism? Many Jews say that the Torah, which they believe God dictated to Moses, teaches them how to live a life of purpose and value. It is the most important text in Judaism, and it is often read out in synagogues, where Jews go to pray.

ABRAHAM

Abraham is an ancient name in Judaism, Christianity and Islam. The man himself was highly respected and revered in all three major world faiths.

His birth name was Abram. But God is said to have renamed him Abraham, meaning 'father of many', and appointed him his messenger on earth.

To the Jews, Abraham gave the covenant, an agreement that revealed to the people the close relationship between them and God. It strengthened their faith in God. It also told them about the creation of living beings, the renewal of creation after the Great Flood and the birth of the Jews, the chosen people of God.

To the Christians, Abraham was a model of saintliness. Jesus Christ was said to be a direct descendant of Abraham. Their religious faith was rooted in Abraham, whom they considered their godfather.

In Islam, too, Abraham is said to be one of the ancestors of Muhammad the Prophet, and therefore held in high regard.

Abraham's deep faith in God gave him incredible spiritual strength. He decried idol worship. He advised those who worshipped the sun and moon not to pray to elements that change or mutate. The one true God is always constant and protects humankind at all times. Abraham obeyed every one of God's commands unquestioningly. He was even ready to sacrifice his son Isaac when He commanded it. Of course, God did not actually want Abraham to go through with it; He was only testing Abraham's faith.

Abraham's devotion to God moulded him into a righteous and compassionate individual. He remained a man of peace through his life. He was known to his followers as a special friend of God, through whom they could approach the almighty.

At the same time, Abraham was detested by idol worshippers. They wanted to get rid of him, so they built a massive fire once to burn him to death. But the fire became so huge that no one could go near it. How would they ever throw Abraham into it? Finally, they tied him up and catapulted him right into the roaring flames. But his faith in the almighty kept him safe even then. Only the ropes that tied him got burnt.

The three religious faiths that revered him worshipped God under different names. Abraham, however, made it clear that names and forms are man-made, and that God is the same for all.

THE SOWER AND THE SEED

The people of Israel gathered on the shores of the Sea of Galilee to hear Jesus speak. They sat down wherever they could, on hard rocks, on green grass or on dry soil, and waited for Jesus to address them. The sun shone overhead and a few birds flew in the skies.

A broad smile lit up Jesus's kind face. He wore his dark hair and beard roughly cropped. His deep-set, compassionate brown eyes scanned the crowd. He began to speak, and he spoke just like everyone else, so the crowd immediately felt at ease.

'Tell me, who among you is a sower?' Jesus asked. Several people raised their hands. They were poor farmers who owned small pieces of land.

Jesus continued, 'Once, a farmer bought a large piece of land. It was partly rocky, partly covered with thorny bushes and partly fertile. He then brought a big bag of seeds and began sowing. As he walked around sprinkling the seeds in the soil, some seeds fell on the path. Birds swooped down and ate them up. Some fell on the rocky ground with scant soil. These seeds sprouted after a shower or two. But when the sun shone, the young plants wilted because the rocks prevented their roots from going deep enough.

'Some other seeds fell among thorny bushes. They sprouted and began to grow. But soon, they were choked by the bushes and could not grow any more.

'The seeds that fell on good soil grew well and yielded grain. Some plants yielded more and some less.'

Jesus stopped speaking. He rubbed his hands and looked around at the listeners. No one moved. None spoke. All of them simply watched Jesus, a questioning look on their faces. After a while, they began to whisper among themselves. The whispers grew into a murmur. Some shook their heads and frowned. Others nodded. Finally they got up, a few at a time, and gradually dispersed.

The sun was in the western sky and a gentle breeze blew from the Sea of Galilee. Jesus's disciples now surrounded him. They said, 'Many have not understood what you wanted to convey. Sowing seeds is an everyday affair. So why make a story of it they are wondering. Should we go and discuss it with them?'

Jesus laughed and asked, 'Are you sure *you* have understood?' Without waiting for their reply, he continued, 'The seed is the message. The sower is the messiah, who brings the message to the people. The soil is the people's mind and the growth of the plant indicates how much the mind has understood. Some of them, like the seeds that fell on the path, hear my teachings, but the words have no effect on them.

'Some others listen a little more sincerely, but they don't understand much. So they forget, like the seeds on the rocky soil.

'Then there are those who listen even more attentively and understand. But once they are back home, the joys and sorrows of family life and other relationships envelop them and the message is gone from their minds – just like the seeds that were choked by the thorny bushes.

'There is one more group of people, who, like the seeds that fell on good soil, understand and remember what they have understood, some more, some less. They are the ones who really benefit, according to the depth of their understanding. They bring joy and sunshine into their lives and to others around them.'

The disciples went out and discussed the parable with the people over several days, patiently answering their questions.

Jesus was happy.

'Are you sure the people will follow your teachings?' his disciples asked.

Jesus smiled. 'Yes and no,' he replied. 'We will have to wait and see. Stories are amazing. You might not understand their value immediately, but your mind thinks about them until, one day, they make sense.'

There is a difference between parables and stories. Stories can be long or short, and usually fun all the way. Parables are short. They can make you blink or they can make you think. You may wonder and ponder, discuss and debate, till the intended meaning of the parable shows up.

Jesus wove his parables with examples from the simple, day-to-day lives of people to make it easier for them to connect to the underlying message.

A CAT FOR THE MICE

In a busy town, there once lived a man who wanted to be a spiritual seeker, and so he went in search of a teacher. After a long search he found one and sought his guidance. With patience and dedication, he learnt from his guru the essentials of spirituality* and spiritual practice.

Back home, he found his mind constantly bombarded with the distractions of the world. His desires were many, and this situation was totally unsuitable for the kind of spirituality that he was trying to acquire. He, therefore, decided to leave his town and go in search of a quieter environment without any distractions.

So, the seeker said goodbye to his parents and stepped out of the house. He did not turn back, and he did not hesitate. He proceeded briskly till he reached a quiet, wooded region. He liked the calm atmosphere

*The quality of being concerned with the soul or something greater than the self, and not material things

of the place and promptly settled down there. Sitting under the shade of a tree, he began to quieten his mind. There was nothing to disturb him and he found peace descending on him. He was happy. He thanked his guru in his mind and began to meditate.

A few days passed. One morning he found his washed loincloth, which had been hanging on the branch of a tree for drying, torn to shreds and nibbled by rats. This disturbed him greatly. How could he manage short of one loincloth?

He could not meditate. He kept thinking about his loincloth and how to prevent rats from getting at it. At last, he decided to get a cat. It would keep the rats away. He postponed his meditation and went in search of a cat.

The cat he procured made a feast of the rats at night and his loincloth was saved!

The following night, too, there were no rats since the cat kept vigil. Once again, the loincloth was saved, but the cat had lost his dinner. He mewed hungrily. How to feed the cat was a question the seeker had to answer. Once more his meditation was disturbed. He decided that to bring back his peace of mind he had to buy a cow so he could feed the cat milk.

The cat was happy, the loincloth was saved, but the seeker had no time for his meditation. Milking the cow and looking after it was time-consuming.

His agitated mind searched for a solution. Something had to be done to regain his meditation time.

He then went in search of a girl who would marry him and look after the cow, the cat *and* him. He could then meditate in peace.

The seeker's mission was a success. He met a beautiful girl, who agreed to be his wife and maintain the household, allowing him to carry on with his spiritual practice peacefully.

The seeker, at last, breathed a sigh of relief and resumed his spiritual routine properly. But not for long.

In just a few short months, his wife was with child. The seeker had to look after her during her pregnancy, get her nutritious food to eat and take her to the doctor from time to time. He did not mind missing his meditation and being in the service of his wife because he was looking forward to the birth of his baby.

After nine long months, a healthy baby girl was born. The father was tempted to spend all his waking hours with the baby. Meditation was forgotten.

The seeker now found that, in order to bring up the child, it was no longer possible to live in his present surroundings. Going back to his town was the only option.

With a nice home and a loving wife, the seeker became a householder in every sense of the word.

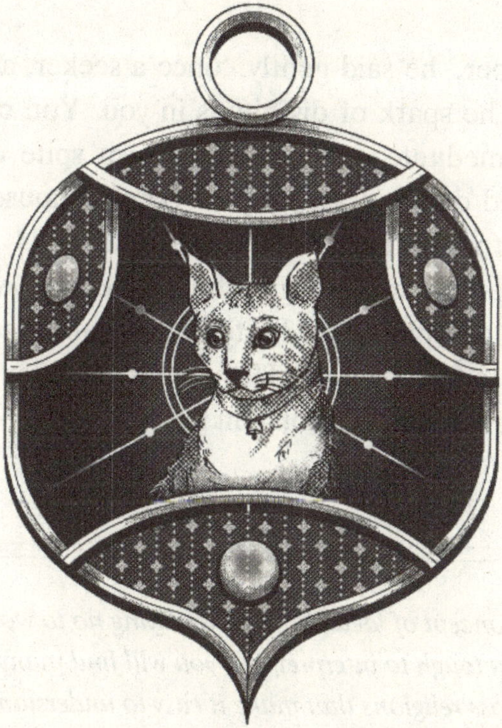

Spiritual practice was no longer possible. There was not a minute to spare for meditation.

One day, he met his guru at the temple. The sight of his disciple holding a child in his arms astonished him. Before he could say anything, the guilty disciple confessed. The guru remarked, laughingly, 'You started as a seeker and have now become a family man – all because of your desire to protect your loincloth.' The seeker hung his head in silence.

The guru paused, patted the baby's cheek and gave his disciple one last piece of advice before he left.

'Remember,' he said gently, 'once a seeker, always a seeker. The spark of divinity is in you. You can find time to meditate and be at peace in spite of your household duties, I assure you. Being a householder will not stop you from being a seeker as well.'

The disciple nodded gratefully. The guru went his way. The disciple had to hasten homewards because it was time to feed his baby. He held his daughter warmly and went home with a song on his lips.

The concept of 'detachment', or saying no to worldly desires, is tough to interpret, but you will find many stories across religions that make it easy to understand.

ADI SHANKARA

Shankara was born in the village of Kalady in Kerala sometime in the seventh century CE. His father died when he was barely seven years old. His mother sent him to a gurukul, where he excelled as a student, studying different schools of philosophy (the study of the nature of knowledge and reality). Religious scholars praised his keen insight and philosophic genius. The king of the region offered him great honour and wealth.

But honour and wealth held no charm for Shankara. His calling was different. He was not going to be a man of the world. He developed an intense desire to renounce the world and become a sanyasi with nothing to call his own except his orange robe and a begging bowl. He wanted to re-establish the Vedic religion, which believed in celebrating the miracle of

Creation and learning about the Creator, to whom all living beings belong.

Shankara's mother was devastated. She wanted her son to be married and have children. She was reluctant to let him leave home.

One day, Shankara and his mother went to the riverside as usual to have a bath. When he stepped into the river, a crocodile caught hold of his leg and dragged him deeper. Shankara screamed.

'Mother,' he cried, 'I'm dying! Please allow me to adopt the life of a sanyasi. It would mean a new lease on life. The crocodile will then spare me.'

Shankara's mother had no choice but to say yes.

The crocodile released Shankara. His life was saved, but his mother had lost him. She bade him a tearful farewell. He assured her that he would be at her side when she breathed her last, and with that promise, he left home.

Shankara met his guru, Govindapada, on the bank of the River Narmada. Govindapada initiated his disciple into *sanyasa* and taught him invaluable lessons. It was a sacred guru-*shishya* relationship.

After leaving his guru, Shankara travelled on foot across the country, teaching his own philosophy, called Advaita, which said that all humans are one, regardless of their caste or creed.

Shankara arrived in Varanasi, the greatest centre of learning and philosophy of those times. Here he spent time explaining and documenting different scriptures. He also wrote a number of devotional poems in praise of God, which are widely chanted and sung by people to this day.

One day, Shankara was going with his disciples to the riverside for a bath, when he came face to face with a *chandala*, an outcaste. The disciples sternly told the man to get out of the way and not pollute the holy path of the guru. The man smiled and said to Shankara, 'I thought your philosophy of Advaita was about the oneness of humankind, with no place for caste or creed, provided there is purity and devotion in the heart. How, then, do you consider me less pure than you?'

Shankara realized his mistake. He composed five beautiful verses on the spot for the man, explaining his philosophy and accepting the man as his guru for awakening him.

Shankara set up four centres in the towns of Puri, Dwaraka, Badrinath and Sringeri to spread his philosophy. Even today they exist as places of learning and devotion. The acharyas, or teachers, in charge of the centres are known as Shankaracharyas. Shankara himself is known as Adi Shankara, or the first Shankara. Thousands of devotees visit these centres to keep themselves on the spiritual path that Shankara paved.

At the age of 32, Shankara went to Kedarnath, in the snowy Himalayas, and merged with the Supreme. He was lost to the world.

Adi Shankara played a prominent role in the cultural history of India as a philosopher and teacher. His work to improve people's lives can never be forgotten.

THE TAILORBIRD AND THE MONKEY

Once, Mahavira noticed his disciples bickering. They taunted each other all the time. This gave rise to anger and bitterness, which, he feared, would lead to violence. And non-violence was one of Mahavira's most important teachings.

One evening, he decided to tell a story. His disciples gathered around eagerly, wondering what this story had to do with what they were learning.

The master began, 'In a forest, there lived a tailorbird and a monkey. One day, the tailorbird noticed clouds gathering in the western sky. She knew the rains were coming, so she lost no time in building a nest to protect herself. She stitched together two thick leaves hanging from a branch with the fibre and cotton that she'd gathered from far and near. She layered this cup-shaped nest with whatever soft materials she could gather.

'The monkey, on the other hand, was not bothered at all. He made fun of the tailorbird.

'"You're wasting your time, little bird! Look at me – I'm not going to let a little rain come in the way of having fun." And off he went, leaping from one tree to the other, cackling away.

'The bird was annoyed, but she continued to build her nest quietly and diligently. Every now and then, the monkey would come back to mock and tease her some more.

'Suddenly, one day, the dark clouds burst into rain. Lightning flashed, the skies thundered and rain poured down in sheets.

'The tailorbird quickly flew into her cosy nest and kept herself warm and dry. The monkey frantically looked for shelter, but there was none anywhere around. He was completely and thoroughly drenched. Shivering, he crouched under the tree, but the rain managed to find him even there.

'The tailorbird peeped out of her nest and saw the monkey huddled under the tree, his teeth chattering. It was now her turn to tease and taunt him. All the anger that she had bottled up inside her came out.

'"What do you have to say for yourself now? You spent all summer having fun while I worked hard. But now I'm perfectly dry and safe, and you're

soaking wet and miserable. Who's the stupid one now, huh?"

'The monkey bared his teeth. In a fit of rage he leapt up in the air and tore the nest apart.

'Now *both* the bird and the monkey were drenched. They repented, but their repentance did no good. Both were shivering in the rain.'

In Jainism, Tirthankaras are teachers who are born human but attain a state of enlightenment in their lives. Mahavira was the 24th Tirthankara. When he was about 30 years old, he renounced his possessions and became a sage, living in exile for 12 whole years, after which he spread the word of Jainism. He was a strong believer in non-violence and truth.

THE TWO BLESSINGS

Long ago, there was a village in the Lahore province of the Delhi Sultanate, which was populated by both Hindus and Muslims. One day it shot into prominence because of the birth of an amazing baby boy. At the time of his birth, the mud hut where he was born was flooded with light. People gathered to see the baby.

The Hindus who saw him exclaimed, 'Great is our Lord Vishnu. The baby has a divine countenance. Praise the lord!'

When Muslims saw him, they declared, 'He is a noble child blessed by almighty Allah!'

Though Hindu by birth, young Nanak was equally loved by Muslims. The spark of divinity in him attracted everybody, no matter what their religion.

When he was 11 years old, Nanak's parents decided to have his thread ceremony. The sacred thread would go across his chest in ritualistic grandeur. He would then be initiated into the life of a *dwija*,

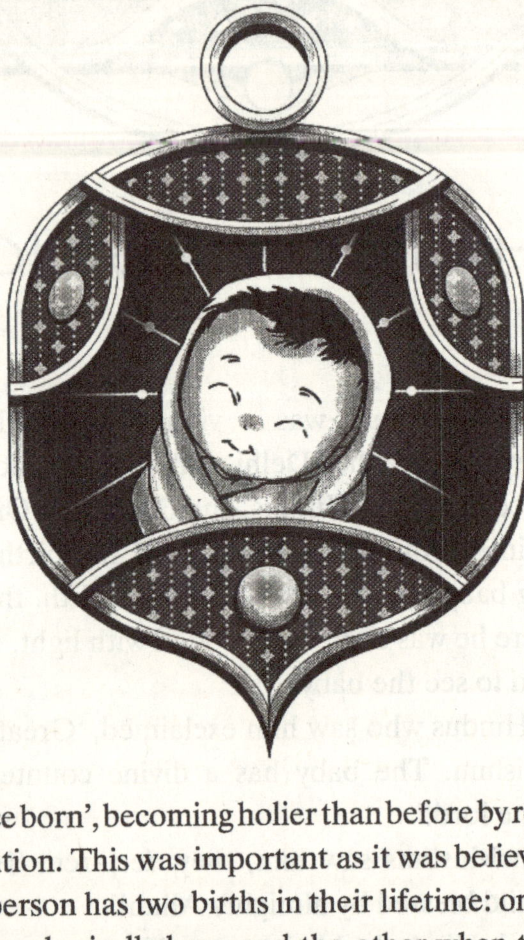

or 'twice born', becoming holier than before by religious convention. This was important as it was believed that every person has two births in their lifetime: one when they are physically born and the other when they are spiritually born after the sacred ceremony.

All the arrangements were made and the most learned priests in the land had been invited to perform the ceremony. Friends and family thronged the place, but Nanak was nowhere to be seen. The auspicious moment for the ceremony to commence was fast approaching. People ran helter-skelter trying to find him.

Where *was* Nanak?

Nanak was walking towards his father's fields. Nanki, his elder sister, spotted him. She grabbed his arm and pulled him back.

'Nanak! Have you taken leave of your senses? We need to go back right now. Everyone is waiting for you,' she cried.

Nanak looked at her. 'Where should I go?' he asked her calmly.

'This is no time to ask silly questions,' said Nanki impatiently and dragged him along.

Nanak loved his sister. For her sake, he went with her.

When the chief priest saw him approaching, he cried excitedly, 'Come, my boy. Time is running out!'

Without a word, Nanak went up to the chief priest and said softly, 'I will wear the sacred thread only on one condition.'

The priest was taken aback. 'And what is that condition, may I ask?' he asked, irritated.

Nanak's answer to the priest (which has now become a famous hymn) shocked the entire assembly. He said:

'Let compassion be your cotton.

Spin it into a yarn of contentment,

Give it knots of restraint
And twists of truth.
Thus will it become a sacred thread for the soul.
If such a one you have,
Then put it on me.'

The silence that followed was heavy. No one spoke a word. Not an eye blinked.

Then, piercing the stunned silence, came Nanak's father's voice, 'The ceremony is off. Before leaving, the priests and everyone else may partake of the food sanctified by Nanak's enlightened words.'

***

The veneration for Guru Nanak (as he came to be known) grew over the years. There was none that doubted the purity of his heart.

But there was an undercurrent of hostility among the two religious sects, which Guru Nanak sensed.

He told them that there was only one God, who treated all people as equal; there was no Hindu or Muslim in His eyes. No differences could come in the way of worshipping Him.

Doubtful eyes stared at him. Was he a Hindu or a Muslim, they wondered. Guru Nanak said, 'All religions have the same message. They are different paths leading to the same goal.' Some listeners seemed to agree. There were others who frowned at his words and vehemently disagreed with him.

This won't do, thought Guru Nanak. *There must be some way to unite people*. After a lot of deliberation, he finally found a way. He carefully extracted the essence of both Hindu and Muslim scriptures and blended them into a comprehensive whole. He called this Sikhism and raised the slogan of 'Ik Onkar' or 'God is one'. His followers came to be known as Sikhs.

Guru Nanak's disciples were both Hindus and Muslims. His closest disciple, Bhai Mardana, was a Muslim. But none of them claimed to be Hindu or Muslim. They were Sikhs, united by the universal thought of 'Ik Onkar'.

For many years, Guru Nanak, along with some of his followers, travelled far and wide, spreading the message of peace and of the one supreme reality.

Sometimes they travelled weary distances across arid lands and dense forests before they came upon a place to rest. On one such occasion, tired from their journey, they were happy to reach a village with green fields, fruit-laden trees and well-dressed people. The disciples were excited.

'May I go and request the people for some food and shelter?' Bhai Mardana asked and waited impatiently for his guru to nod. He then ran to the nearest door and knocked. As soon as it was opened, he said, 'A few of us are travelling with our guru, Nanak Saheb. We are hungry and have not found a bed to sleep on for several days. Can you kindly –' But before Bhai Mardana could finish, the door was shut in his face. The rest of the villagers were equally rude.

'Guru Nanak is great. You will be blessed by serving him,' Bhai Mardana shouted in the marketplace. But no one stopped to listen to him.

One man remarked in an unkind tone, 'Go to the town hall. Brush away the ants and insects on the floor and lie down. You may find some food there left over by previous travellers.'

'Such heartless people…' Bhai Mardana muttered, gnashing his teeth.

'No need for such comments,' Guru Nanak chided him gently and proceeded to the town hall. It was a sleepless, hungry night for the travellers.

In the morning, they left the village. Before going away, Bhai Mardana wanted to scream at the villagers for their nasty behaviour. But before he could do that, Guru Nanak turned to them, raised his hand and said softly, 'May you all be blessed and continue living well in the village.' His disciples looked at him in speechless astonishment.

'Has Guruji gone crazy?' they wondered.

Guru Nanak just smiled.

The journey continued, and soon the travellers reached another village. This village did not look as prosperous as the previous one.

Nevertheless, with some trepidation, Bhai Mardana asked at a cottage, 'We are weary travellers. We haven't eaten or slept for several days. Can you kindly host us?'

To his great surprise, the villager was all too ready to host them. 'It is a blessing to look after guests,' he said and invited them in. He washed their tired feet and gave them tender coconut water to drink. Fresh food was cooked for them, and everyone had a comfortable place to sleep.

Early the next morning, Guru Nanak began to sing bhajans in his melodious voice. The villagers gathered round him and listened with great joy.

Soon it was time to leave. The villagers bade them a fond farewell. Once again, Guru Nanak turned to them before leaving and blessed them.

'May you be blessed to leave your village and travel far and wide,' he said.

Once again, the disciples were bewildered. They looked at him, their eyes pleading for clarification. But he said nothing.

For days, the disciples kept thinking about their master's extraordinary blessings for the two villages, till, at last, Bhai Mardana came up with an explanation.

On hearing it, Guru Nanak said, 'Well done, son. Thinking deeply with a sincere effort to find a solution always helps.'

From then on, the followers of Nanak Saheb took his words more seriously and dwelt upon them. Hindu–Muslim hostility slowly evaporated. They formed a united brotherhood.

So what was Bhai Mardana's explanation for Guru Nanak's two different blessings?

'In the first village, if Guruji had blessed them to travel, their unpleasant nature would infect others, whereas if the people of the second village travelled, they would make the world a better place to live in.'

Guru Nanak believed that three main principles could guide people in their lives: keeping God in mind, living a truthful life, and giving to and caring for others. He established the practice of 'langar' (free community kitchen), which is why gurdwaras – the Sikh place of worship – serve a free meal to any visitor, regardless of their religion, caste or status.

THE MISSING MAN

Once, ten young men set out on an adventure with great excitement. They crossed hills and valleys, dense jungles and thorny pathways. At one point in their journey, they reached a sparkling stream, completely exhausted. They drank the cool water to their fill and sat for a while on the banks of the stream, admiring the beauty all around them.

Soon it was time to continue their travels. The ten young men jumped into the stream and started to swim across it.

When they reached the other side, one of them cried, 'Wait!'

The others raised their eyebrows and looked at him.

'Let's just make sure all of us have crossed the stream safely. I'll count us,' the one who had spoken first said and began counting.

'One...two…nine…' he counted. 'Oh no, we're only nine!'

'What?' shouted the others. 'How's that possible? Where's the tenth?' They looked at each other, completely bewildered. They slumped to the ground, hands on their heads. Some whimpered while others sniffled. Eventually, they all started weeping. 'The tenth one is lost. How can we continue our journey now?' they cried.

Just then, a Zen master passed by. He stopped and asked the adventurers, 'What happened? Why are you all so upset? Is there any way I can help?'

They looked up at him. The one who had counted said, 'You're just an ordinary man. What can you do?'

But the master looked at him expectantly, so finally the man told him about the tragedy that had befallen the group.

The master smiled to himself and said aloud, 'I think I know how to relieve your sorrow.'

The men started at him in disbelief. One of them said, 'Look here! We have counted ourselves and we've even searched for the tenth one in the stream. There's no use!'

Another man demanded, 'How can you bring back someone who has drowned?'

A third man asked doubtfully, 'Do you really believe you can find the tenth one?'

The master nodded.

'Then please do something quickly; bring him back while he's still breathing,' the third man said.

'I can get him back without jumping into the stream,' the master replied calmly.

'Impossible!' the man cried indignantly.

The fourth man, however, decided to give the master a chance. 'Please, sir, go ahead and do what you can to bring our companion back,' he said.

'He's right here amongst you,' said the master.

'What? Show him then!' the fifth man said.

The master made them all stand in a row and counted them.

'One, two, three, four, five, six, seven, eight, nine... ten! So, there you are. Ten young men standing in front of me.'

The sixth man, refusing to believe him, said, 'You are deceiving us.'

'What proof do you have to show that we are ten?' asked the seventh man.

The master replied, 'I'll tap each of you in turn. Cry "Ahoy!" at the tap, and keep count of the ahoys that you hear.'

The men agreed, and sure enough, ten ahoys were heard!

The eighth man said, 'We agree that we are ten now. But tell us – which of us was the tenth one who "got lost"?'

'You,' said the master.

'Wonderful,' cried the man. 'I'm the tenth man and I have been found. Now we are all here. Let us continue our journey.'

The ninth man said, 'Wait. Let me count once again to make sure.'

When he came to the eighth man, the latter said, 'But *I'm* the tenth man. How can you count me as the eighth?'

The ninth man was confused. He turned to the master and said, 'You tried to cheat us! Just leave us alone and go your way.'

The master sighed and turned and was about to leave when one of them fell at his feet and said, 'You are absolutely right, sir! Thank you for helping us. I was the first one to count. After counting nine of us, I did not realize that *I* was the tenth. You have helped me get rid of my ignorance.'

The master walked away happily. He was able to enlighten at least one of the ten young men.

The veil of ignorance covers human existence says Zen Buddhism. This leads to sorrow. Only a few people realize who they truly are. They understand the purpose of life. They live in bliss. But many others are not ready to even take the help of masters who know the truth. For them, life remains sorrowful.

THE KING OF DWARAKA

Krishna belonged to a clan known as the Yadavas. In those days, the Yadavas were treated very badly by other people. It was Krishna who came to their rescue and vowed that he would create a kingdom for them, where they could live with a sense of dignity and honour.

Vishwakarma, the celestial architect, was called to design and build this kingdom. But however would he manage such a task? Vishwakarma was at a loss. Krishna noticed the deep lines of worry that furrowed his forehead. He obviously needed help. Krishna smiled and pointed to the sea in the northwestern region of the country, now known as Gujarat. Vishwakarma nodded. His face cleared and he set to work. He reclaimed the sea, and sea turned to land. He made a kingdom as large as Krishna wanted it to be. In Vishwakarma's deft hands, it became a very beautiful place, comfortable and satisfying in every way for the citizens.

The people adored their king and were utterly devoted to him. Aware of his divine qualities, they considered him God in human form. And Krishna did not disappoint them. He was known as Dwarkadhish, meaning 'the ruler of Dwaraka'.

Krishna's durbar was a grand and beautiful place. Every morning, he would meet his people in the durbar. Some came to pay homage, and he received their offerings with grace. A few came with petitions, and he gave them a patient ear and solved their problems in no time. A good number came just to be close to Krishna. They say, in the scriptures, that Krishna's actions were directed towards the world but he was not of the world. This sense of detachment kept him eternally happy and peaceful. He spread joy around him like ripples in a pond. His honesty put them at ease and they had no feeling of fear or trepidation in his presence, not even children.

One morning, Krishna sat as usual in his court in all his splendour.

Suddenly, a little boy, known as Govinda, burst into the hall. All eyes turned in his direction. Govinda ran up to the throne and, pointing to his right cheek, cried, 'Look, my lord, look!'

There were red fingerprints on his cheek. The boy continued, 'That…that boy Gopala, who I thought was a good friend, slapped me so…so very hard.' He whimpered, blinking back his tears. Uneasiness prevailed in the durbar. Why was the little boy bringing such a trifle to the king's notice?

Everyone expected Krishna to humour the boy briefly and send him off. But he just got up and asked Govinda, 'Where's this naughty boy who slapped you?'

The boy was only too ready to take Krishna to Gopala's house. As if he was seething with anger, Krishna followed the boy briskly. All the others followed the king, bewildered by his reaction.

Govinda led Krishna to the farthest end of the royal road.

Before Krishna could get to the house, someone from the crowd ran ahead and announced, 'The king is coming! God knows what punishment awaits the boy who slapped his friend.'

From the small cottage at the end of the road, Gopala's father came out, palms folded respectfully. He trembled with fright while Gopala stood behind him, trying to hide from the king.

Finally Krishna arrived. Standing akimbo, he held the father's gaze for one long moment. A hush fell.

What would the king do next?

Krishna said to Gopala's father, 'Look what your son has done to his friend.'

And that was all. Krishna turned around and began walking back towards the palace.

The people were amazed, amused and intrigued. Did their mighty king walk all the way just to say these few words? But who could question the king? The people too turned and followed him. Only the complainant stood watching his friend and his father. There were tears rolling down the father's cheeks.

Govinda tugged at Gopala's arm and said, 'Come on! It's all right. My cheek doesn't hurt any more.'

'Thank you,' Gopala said. 'My father is blind. He has always wanted to meet our beloved king. He's shedding tears of joy for having met him now.'

Govinda turned to look at the father again. But he had gone inside the hut. Govinda asked his friend curiously, 'Could your father have seen the king through his blindness?'

'I think so. He tells me that our king is divine.'

The two friends held hands and ran away to play.

All those who have come across this legend have felt that the blind man did see Krishna in his divine splendour.

It is accepted across the seas that the mystery of the relation between the divine and the devotee is strictly between the two of them. No one else knows anything about it.

ZOROASTER

Some four thousand years ago in Persia, there lived a nobleman. He had a large family. One of his sons was named Zoroaster, a gentle boy who cared deeply for his fellow beings.

The Persians of those days followed tribal traditions and worshipped several gods with blind faith. The rituals were many, and people conducted them fanatically, even sacrificing animals to the gods.

But Zoroaster was different. He was against this form of worship. An inner voice kept whispering to him these practices were not right.

When Zoroaster grew up, he became a priest and began to question these age-old traditions. But he was one against so many. How would he steer them to the right path?

One day, Zoroaster had a vision in which a radiant spirit appeared before him.

'I am Good Thought,' the figure said. 'Tell me who you are.'

Zoroaster was taken aback but he answered boldly, 'Zoroaster, enemy of false believers and friend of the righteous.'

Pleased with his answer, the spirit spoke to him, and Zoroaster listened in stunned silence. 'You must oppose blood sacrifices. Let mankind learn about faith and the power of good deeds through you. Be sure to help the poor and the ignorant. They must know that there is only one supreme God – Ahura Mazda.' So saying, the spirit vanished.

When Zoroaster came out of his vision, he was a changed person. From that day he was inspired to preach to the people of Persia. Following the guidance of the spirit, he told them about Ahura Mazda. 'He created mankind and the world and all good things. Whenever evil spirits threaten to destroy his beautiful creations, have faith in him. Good will prevail and evil will be destroyed.'

As more and more people gathered to listen to Zoroaster, he told them, 'Avoid telling lies, support the poor and needy, and live a life of purity and sacrifice. After this life on earth, the good will go to heaven, while the evil-minded will go to hell and suffer. There may be a few neutral ones who will have an ordinary existence, neither joyous nor sorrowful.'

Many opposed his teachings. They did not want him in their midst. Zoroaster retreated into the wilderness for ten years. A few people who loved and respected him followed him, and with them he shared his wisdom.

Zoroaster's teachings formed the basis of the religion that came to be known as Zoroastrianism. It is one of the oldest religions in the world, believing in one God, quite in contrast to the then prevalent tribal faith in many gods. Zoroastrianism was the state religion for three Persian dynasties. Eventually, when Muslims took over and began to spread the faith of Islam, the followers of Zoroastrianism had to move elsewhere. Although the tenets of Zoroaster's religion helped shape Judaism, Christianity and Islam, it was not able to survive in Persia.

Zoroaster passed away at the age of 77, but the religion continued. The Zoroastrians migrated to Pakistan and India. Many of them settled down in the western Indian states of Gujarat and Maharashtra. They are known as Parsis. When asked about their faith, they said, 'Zoroaster taught us to put ourselves wholeheartedly into good deeds, simply for the love and joy of doing them. Being joyous helps us overcome hurdles.'

None of these teachings of Zoroaster were against the prevalent religious thoughts in India. They were, in fact, beneficial to the existing society. Thus, Zoroaster's beliefs continued on, and followers of his principles are still present in modern India.

DRAWN OUT OF THE WATER

The stone quarry was buzzing with activity. Strong hands were heaving out large boulders and carrying them to the site of the pyramid. The men perspired and panted. But they continued to work without a break. The pyramid had to be completed in the next few days. The pharaoh had given them a week's time. He was keeping an eagle eye on the activities from the ramparts of his palace.

The working men, the Hebrews, had been in bondage in Egypt for many long years. They were the slaves of the pharaoh. They were God-fearing men who worked sincerely. The women stayed at home as homemakers.

Deep furrows showed up on the pharaoh's forehead. His thoughts were not happy.

'The Hebrew population is swelling rapidly. What if one day they all decide to leave my land and go somewhere else? Who will build the pyramids then? Who will harvest the wheat and barley?'

The pharaoh became increasingly worried and finally gave a terrible order: 'Have every newborn Hebrew baby boy killed. Their population must be curbed at any cost!'

The ministers were aghast, but they had no choice except to obey their king. They nodded gravely and said, 'That is indeed a good idea. Who else but our great pharaoh could have thought of it?'

A heavy silence followed as the minsters turned and left to do their duty. The pharaoh returned to his chambers, pleased with himself.

But the mission was not successful. The Hebrews were somehow able to shield every newborn baby boy from the soldiers.

Late one night, Jochebed, a devout Hebrew woman, gave birth to a baby boy. She was delighted and frightened at the same time. She carefully kept him hidden away for three months. But one morning, the baby wailed so loudly that the pharaoh's men heard him. Jochebed quickly hid the child in a wooden ark covered with fresh leaves and grass. With tears in her eyes, she gently let the ark down the river Nile. She watched it bob up and down and then disappear downstream. She went back home and prayed sincerely, 'Dear God of my heart, please look after my little one.'

Now, it so happened that the pharaoh's daughter was playing with her friends on the riverbank when she saw the ark.

'How cute! Bring me that ark,' she told one of her playmates. Her joy knew no bounds when she saw the baby inside. She hugged him and kissed him and danced round with him.

'He's mine, my very own. He's Moses!' she cried in delight. Moses meant 'drawn out'.

Moses grew up as the princess's son. He was a happy child. There were many little cousins in the royal family to play with. There was a variety of food to eat at every meal. There were servants at his beck and call.

When Moses grew older, he began to notice some things that he hadn't earlier. He was distinctly taller and sturdier than his cousins and playmates. His skin was darker. He realized that he looked more like the workers, the Hebrews. His curious mind began to think. 'If I do not belong to royalty, why should I be here?' His heart went out to his clan, which was suffering in slavery. He could not wait to join them.

'God, please help me help my people,' he prayed, and then he faced the pharaoh boldly.

'My people, whom you call the Hebrews, will no longer live in Egypt. They have been enslaved and tortured here for long enough. They will travel to a new land, a land they can call their own. In the future, theirs will be a life of freedom,' he announced. And without waiting for the pharaoh's reaction, he joined his people and asked them to pack up.

The Hebrews were overjoyed. They quickly got their things together and streamed out of Egypt, with Moses leading them. They followed him all the way to the Red Sea.

But the pharaoh was not one to sit back and watch. He sent his best soldiers to chase after the Hebrews and bring them back.

At the seashore, the people clung to each other, terrified. Hundreds of soldeirs were close on their heels, and in front lay the great roaring sea. Death faced them on both sides.

'Have faith,' Moses told them. 'Pray. Help will surely come.'

He then faced the sea, threw up his arms, closed his eyes and prayed to God in heaven. With unshaken faith in their leader, whom they considered to be God's representative on earth, the Hebrews waited with hope in their hearts.

All of a sudden, a deafening noise shook the earth. Gigantic waves lashed the seashore and in a few crashing moments the sea parted. It formed two mountains of water on either side, leaving a dry pathway for the people to go through and cross the sea.

There was no time to stand and stare in astonishment. Moses herded the people through the pathway at lightning speed. The Egyptian chariots dashed forward to follow the people. But before they could step on the pathway, the two mountains of waves rolled back and joined together with an ear-splitting noise. The pathway was closed. The chariots fell back. The men rolled over on the sand and the horses neighed in fright.

The Hebrews had crossed the sea safely. They looked up at Moses with awe. His gentle smile put them at ease as he led them on. The tiring journey continued for many days.

Moses showed no signs of fatigue, but he knew that his end was near. The people would have to continue on their own. He took them to the banks of the river Jordan and there he bid them farewell.

The people felt faint. Their faith rested on their leader. Without him they would be like a rudderless boat. Where would they go? What would they do? Moses pacified them and said, 'Do not lose hope. Have faith in the almighty. I obeyed his command to help you so far. Now, you are on your own. Do not forget that He is always with you and will take care of you.'

The people were encouraged by his words. They began to feel confident of themselves. Yes, God would stand by them, but they would have to learn to lead their own lives.

Moses gave the Hebrews the Ten Commandments of God.

'Obey the Lord's commandments, and you will be protected. Carry on till you reach Israel,' he told them and departed.

No sooner did the people face the river than it parted, just as the ocean had parted for them. Chanting praises of the Lord, they crossed the river Jordan and stepped on to the land that would be theirs. Israel. From then on, the Hebrews living in Israel would be known as Israelites. They remembered to obey the Ten Commandments all their lives. Their life of slavery was a thing of the past. Now they were free.

The Ten Commandments are the principles that God laid out for humans according to Judaism and Christianity. They tell us not to steal or be dishonest, and to honour our parents and keep the last, or seventh, day of the week for rest and prayer. In Judaism, this day is Saturday and is called the Sabbath.

THE KING'S BOONS

In the olden days, cattle fairs used to be an annual feature in several Indian villages. The people in the surrounding villages looked forward to them because they could buy and sell cattle and meet their friends at these fairs.

One such fair began before the onset of monsoon in that region. Eager to buy a cow, a farmer had come to the fair from a far-off village. Activities were in full swing as he walked around the fair bargaining for a good cow. By the time he finalized his choice, the day was done, and it was past sunset. The crowd had thinned. The unsold cattle were being driven away. The fair came to a close.

The farmer had a long way to go. Tired and hungry, he coaxed the cow and its calf to walk briskly. He pulled and pushed the cow homewards. But the animal refused to move. The farmer was cursing his misfortune loudly when a wandering sage came by.

'Is there a problem?' the sage asked kindly. The farmer looked at the thin figure in front of him and was not impressed. But he needed help, so he told the sage about the cow's stubbornness. Without a word, the sage picked up the little calf standing close to its mother and began walking. The cow mooed and quietly followed him. The surprised farmer walked along silently.

To distract himself from the eeriness of the enveloping darkness, the farmer decided to talk to the sage.

'What do you do for a living?' he asked.

'The world looks after me,' replied the sage and in turn, asked the farmer, 'do you pray to God for the things you need?'

'I do. Sometimes my prayers are answered, and sometimes not,' the farmer replied.

'There are ways to have your wishes fulfilled – like the way a simple solution was found to make the cow walk,' the sage said, his eyes twinkling.

'And what are they?' asked the farmer eagerly.

The sage laughed and said, 'Let me tell you a story. There was once a king who wanted to see what his kingdom was like in the night. So, one dark night, he wore a disguise and got on his horse, his bodyguards following him some distance away. Unfortunately, he was captured by some dacoits on a lonely road. They were ready to hurt him if he did not part with whatever he had, including his horse. Just then, five young men returning from a late-night celebration stopped in front of the dacoits, fought them and drove them away even before the king's bodyguards arrived on the scene.

'Pleased with the men, the king revealed his identity and invited them to the court the following day so he could reward each of them with a boon.

'The young men were terribly excited. All night they thought and thought about what boons they would ask for.

'The next day, they presented themselves at the king's court dressed in their best clothes. The courtiers looked at the brave young men in awe, wondering what they would ask for.

'The first of them spoke with great humility and said, "Your Majesty! There are no good roads connecting our village to other parts of the kingdom. We have a tough time going to and fro especially in the rainy season. I would like to have the roads paved."

'"Done," said the king and turned to the second young man. The latter wished to have a better house to live in since his present one was in a wretched state. The king gave him a mansion.

'The third man said, "Your Majesty, I live with my ageing mother. She finds it difficult to look after our household. May I request you to grant her helping hands to make her tasks easier?"

'The king readily agreed to provide him with a cook, a gardener, a maid and a handyman. The fourth man was the youngest. He was a little hesitant to speak. The king gently encouraged him to say what was on his mind. Finally, the young man blushed and said softly that he would like to be married.

'The king laughed and said, "My sister's pretty daughter is on the lookout for a worthy husband. Why don't you meet her?"

'The last of the young men was quiet for a while. As the king looked at him expectantly, he said in a clear voice, "I have nothing to demand for myself."

'"Oh – what would you like me to do then?" asked the bewildered king.

'The man continued, "Your Majesty, I would like you to spend a night in my house as my guest once every six months."

'The king was taken aback. So were the courtiers. No one had ever made such a request. Nevertheless, the king agreed. Such a harmless request was not to be rejected.

'However, to fulfil this boon, the king's government had to do some work. Firstly, for the king to travel in comfort, the road from the palace to the man's house needed to be well paved.

'Secondly, a well-furnished, comfortable home was a basic requirement if the king had to spend a night there. So the young man was provided with a luxurious home.

'For the home to be well maintained, a retinue of servants was employed.

'Lastly, the youth's marriage to a good-natured girl was arranged, so that the king could be well looked after during his stay.'

The sage stopped and looked at the farmer.

'Incredible!' exclaimed the farmer with a sigh. 'Asking for one boon and receiving along with it all the boons that had been granted to his companions!'

'So, my friend,' the sage advised the farmer, 'when we ask for this or that from the divine, those wishes may or may not be granted, but if we ask for the greatest boon of all, the others will come on their own.'

The sage and the farmer walked the rest of the way in silence. The sage gently let the calf down at the farmer's doorstep and it ran to its mother. He then turned and went his way.

In ancient India, wandering sages or sadhus were not an uncommon sight. They're often mentioned in mythology as well as folklore, from which it is known that they were generally devotees of Shiva and led a life of austerity, detached from worldly attractions. Their matted hair, ashen skin and minimal clothing made most people keep away from them. For the few who happened to interact with them, they had interesting advice to give about life and living it the right way.

SWAMI VIVEKANANDA

'Arise! Awake! And stop not till the goal is reached!' Nineteenth-century India echoed with these words of Swami Vivekananda, an extraordinary spiritual leader. He was a very popular figure with the youth of India, and his message of an eternal quest for truth was an ideal they all aspired to.

He believed in young people's ability to achieve great things and in their capacity to do their best. He taught them how to become better people. His contributions were so great that his birthday was declared as National Youth Day.

While Vivekananda often addressed the youth because they were the future of the country, he also spoke to others about God.

To the oft-asked question 'Where is God?' he would reply, 'God can be found in your own heart and in all other living beings.' He said that you could not believe in God until you learnt to believe in yourself.

Vivekananda was born on 12 January 1893. His parents named him Narendranath. His father was a successful and forward-thinking lawyer, and his mother, a homemaker, was a woman of great moral strength and devotion. The child Naren was precocious and full of energy. His mother found him so restless and uncontrollable that she sometimes lamented, 'I prayed to God for a son and he has sent me one of his demons instead!'

Naren was attracted to the wandering monks he met in his childhood and liked to practise meditation. His father saw to it that he had a good education, and Naren excelled in his studies, as well as in music, gymnastics and oratory.

At the threshold of youth, he went through a spiritual crisis and was assailed by doubts about God, worship and religious practices. That was the time he met his guru, Sri Ramakrishna Paramahansa. He patiently cleared Naren's doubts by reasoning them out and giving him practical examples. Narendranath was overwhelmed. The guru won over his disciple through pure, unselfish love. Thus began a guru-disciple relationship unique in the history of spiritual masters.

Fired by spiritual ideals, Narendranath took the vows of a monk, donned ochre robes and became Swami Vivekananda.

Vivekananda wandered across India experiencing many hardships that made his human and spiritual values stronger. His travels helped him develop a deeper understanding of the meaning of religion. He realized that true religion was far from just ritualistic practices. Moreover, a true monk not only practises meditation and other spiritual rituals but also puts himself generously at the service of humanity. He understood that religion should mean tolerance, compassion and universal acceptance. Such in-depth study and experience gave him the courage and conviction to talk boldly about India and its religious attitudes at the World Parliament of Religions in America in 1893. He was given a standing ovation for his speech. He credited his success to Sri Ramakrishna's blessings and his beloved motherland, which had taught him the core values of human existence.

Back in India he worked tirelessly to establish a monastic order called the Ramakrishna Mission. Here, he strove to put his ideas into practice. He served the needy in every possible way, providing them with education, hospitals and relief in times of natural disasters as well as giving them spiritual solace.

'The history of the world is the history of the dedicated men who have faith in themselves and work selflessly,' he told his fellow monks. They tirelessly carried on the work of the mission.

Unfortunately, Vivekananda's health began to fail him when he was still very young; he died when he was just 39 years old. But the momentum he set up during his lifetime keeps the mission going to this day.

THE BARGAIN

An elderly mullah was in charge of teaching children to recite verses from the Quran. His appearance commanded respect. He was tall and wore a short beard. A white skull cap covered his bald head partially, and his dark eyes proclaimed his wisdom. When his deep voice started reciting, the children joined in the recitation with great reverence. Their bodies swayed backwards and forwards as they spoke in unison. One day, after reciting the verses that had already been taught to them, they stopped and looked up at their teacher. Clearing his throat, the teacher recited a new verse slowly and clearly. The children repeated after him. Once, twice, thrice.

The teacher then told the children the meaning of the new verse. 'Those who give what they have to the cause of Allah are like a grain of corn that grows seven ears, and each ear yields a hundred more grains. To them Allah gives back in the same way.' The children quietly pondered over the meaning of the verse.

'Done for the day. We'll meet next Friday and continue,' said the teacher. He noticed that the children were unusually excited as they dispersed. He overheard what they murmured.

'We'll get back seven hundred times...we'll be rolling in wealth...we can enjoy our lives...'

The teacher's face fell. 'They've misunderstood the verse,' he thought. 'During the next class, I will explain the right meaning with the help of a parable.'

The following Friday, the class recited the new verse well.

'Good job,' the teacher said. 'Now for a story.'

The children were delighted. They closed their books and sat up straight. The teacher began, 'Listen carefully. You'll have to answer a question at the end in order for me to finish the story properly.'

He continued, 'There was once a person who recited this verse, listened to its meaning and went home thinking about it. All night he thought about it. As soon as he got up in the morning, he gathered all his wealth and made a calculation.

'"If I give all of this away in the name of Allah, He will multiply it seven hundred times and give it back to me. This works out to one thousand dinars. Incredible...but it must be true! The teacher said so. It will last me a lifetime," he said to himself. He went to the imam immediately and gave away all his wealth.

'The dismayed imam cried, "Hold it! You need to give away only a portion of your earnings. So say our scriptures." But the man didn't listen.

'"It is for Allah," he declared and walked away.

'When he got home, he was hungry. There was nothing in his kitchen save a small olive and a piece of dry bread, hardly enough to satisfy his hunger. He could not go out and buy food. He had no money.

'He went to bed but did not sleep. He was alert. Allah might choose any moment to shower him with a thousand dinars. But nothing happened.

'When day dawned he decided to remind Allah of the thousand dinars He owed him. He prayed fervently the whole day. Nothing happened. Hunger gnawed at the poor, prayerful man's stomach.

'"Perhaps praying inwardly does not work. Maybe I have to shout to Allah to attract His attention," he thought. He went out of his house to shout to Allah.

'But he cautioned himself. "Wait! I can't let others hear my plea. I must go to an isolated place." So he walked a long distance till he came to a deserted area. There was just a lone tree for shade, and he sat under it. He cleared his throat, threw up his arms, looked up at the heavens and was about to shout out when he saw a person staggering towards him.

'The madman stammered in a loud voice, "Ah... Allah! Your Prophet Muhammad brought Your mess...

message of peace and...and unity. But...but people just keep fighting...fighting. No peace...no unity. You... you lied. And...and I shall punish you for it."

'Dead scared, our poor man quickly climbed up the tree and hid himself. But when the madman drew his sword, he jumped down from the tree and shouted, "Wait! You cannot do that to Allah now. He owes me a thousand dinars." The shocked madman swayed and fell down with a thud. His eyes rolled up and he collapsed.

'The next moment, our poor man's hands grabbed at the dead man's clothes.

'"I'll sell these clothes to buy some bread and wait for Allah...' His voice trailed off as he found a purse in the pocket of the dead man's shirt. He greedily pulled it out and feverishly counted the money in it. It added up to a thousand dinars.

'He breathed a big sigh of relief, looked up and cried, "Well, Allah! You *have* kept Your word. I thank You for it from the bottom of my heart. But remember, I had to save Your life before that."'

The children burst out laughing.

The teacher said, 'Well, dear children. You have enjoyed the story. Now, can you tell me if Allah gave him a reply?'

The children looked at each other. There was a puzzled silence. After a little while, one voice said shyly, 'Allah is not what the man thinks He is.'

'Good,' the teacher said. 'Any other answers?'

Another voice rang out, a little more boldly, 'Saving Allah's life... It was a silly thing to say.'

'Quite right,' said the teacher, smiling.

Finally, he told the students, 'The whole story happened because the man misunderstood the verse. It emphasizes the importance of charity, but not to the extent of giving away everything and feeling lost. The exaggeration picturized in the verse is to make us remember the virtue of charity.' The children looked less puzzled now.

Soon, the class was dismissed. The children ran home laughing over the poor man's plight. At the same time, they made up their minds to give something to charity whenever possible and also to learn the meaning of the verses of the Quran with care.

The verse that the teacher read out to his students is from the longest chapter of the Quran, the holy book of Islam.

THE PHOENIX IN THE SKY

Day broke in the clear Grecian skies. But it was not the usual gentle dawn. It was unusually bright.

As time ticked on, it became brighter and brighter. Brighter than a hundred suns! And the people wondered what sort of magic was afoot.

But soon, the sun lost its brilliance as something more radiant appeared in the sky. The dazzling glow made everyone's eyes water. Yet the people watched, blinking up at the sky.

After a while, they could not stand the extraordinary phenomenon any longer. They feared a catastrophe and prayed fervently to the sun god Ra. They ran to the shrine of the oracle and begged the high priestess to ask the gods what was going on. The oracle raised her hands heavenwards and uttered strange sounds. The people trembled and waited. At last, she turned to them and said, 'The sun god says that his representative, the phoenix, is descending to earth to remind you of the magic and mystery of the natural world, which you must respect.'

Just as the priestess finished talking, a melodious, classical tune filled the air. The awestruck people stood dumbfounded as tongues of flame burst forth from atop a tall tree in the eastern horizon. A huge bird with a fabulous red-and-gold plumage emerged from the flames and soared with perfect grace, in total harmony with the song.

As the day advanced, the phoenix drifted in the sky from east to west. There was not a single soul that did not watch the wonderful spectacle.

All the birds on earth gathered to see the phoenix. They forgot to chirp or even flutter their wings. They were all just still and silent. Animals, from the biggest to the smallest, reptiles, from the longest to the tiniest, fishes in waterbodies, sharks in the sea, and all other living creatures just stopped and watched.

As the day came to a close, a flame burst forth in a tree. The gigantic bird flew to it and settled upon this pyre to be consumed by the flame. While it disappeared from view it sang a song of surprising sweetness. The earth was veiled in silent sadness. Life came to a standstill. Darkness swallowed the sky.

At the first sign of morning light, the earth was born to a new life. The phoenix appeared once again

in all its glory from the eastern flame. The sky was lit up again. The people, joyful, yet perplexed, turned to the high priestess of the oracle.

She declared, 'The phoenix has brought us hope. The future is bright; all we have to do is live harmoniously. We may not get to see the phoenix again. But it will remain as a grand symbol of immortality. As long as earth exists, birth and death will go on. Changes are to be celebrated, not feared.'

The voice died down. The people remained quiet as it echoed in their hearts. They went back home with a feeling of joyful fulfilment. The other creatures resumed their daily routine with renewed enthusiasm.

The phoenix has figured in ancient Chinese, Egyptian and Greek mythology. It brought the message of peace, joy and harmony to the world. Somewhere down the centuries, the story of the legendary bird was forgotten until spiritual masters felt the world desperately needed to hear its message of unity again.

LAO TZU

Unique is the life of Lao Tzu. Universal are his thoughts.

But who was Lao Tzu? He was the founder of one of the greatest religions in the world, Taoism, and the creator of one of the greatest books of wisdom – the *Tao Te Ching*, written for the good of all humankind.

Lao Tzu's mother, it is said, nurtured him lovingly in her womb for 81 long years in a small village in ancient China. Legend says that he came into the world in his 82nd year, born with snow-white hair and a silky beard. He had large ears and dark eyes that were shaded by bushy grey eyebrows. From the day of his birth, he was a healthy man in his 80s who could talk to animals and birds and was blessed with extraordinary wisdom.

When he was born, Lao Tzu's mother saw nine fiery dragons descend from heaven to wash the body of the newborn. Contrary to how fierce they looked, they behaved gently. She instantly recognized the greatness of her son and thanked God with all her heart. She named him Lao Tzu, which means 'the old, wise one'.

From birth, Lao Tzu knew the arts of medicine and healing.

The people of his village visited his house and were speechless at the sight of Lao Tzu, who had a bright aura around him. From that day onwards, they began to follow him. They felt joyful and peaceful in his presence.

More and more people followed him and asked him all sorts of questions. Some asked him if he knew the way to heaven.

He told them, 'I made a great effort to find it. I tried and tried but couldn't. Then, one day, while sitting under a tree thinking about it, a dry leaf fell and slowly moved with the wind. The wind blew north and the leaf moved north. The wind blew south and the leaf moved with it. When the wind stopped, the leaf fell gently to the earth. The wind then started again and the leaf rose in the air. Suddenly, I found myself

becoming the dry leaf, and at that time I knew the way to heaven. I was no longer separate from heaven. I became part of heaven.'

The people silently thought about what he'd said. 'Lao Tzu is a wise man. What he says must be true. We are not as clever as he is. We'll understand...surely we'll understand... but slowly...slowly...' they said to themselves.

Wherever Lao Tzu went, he always rode a grey donkey with dreamy eyes and long white ears. He spoke to her lovingly and she always responded with a gentle bray.

One day, his disciples found Lao Tzu vigorously washing his ears with water. He then washed his donkey's ears with equal energy. Bewildered, they asked him, 'What are you doing?'

'I'm washing away the bad words that I sometimes hear. They will affect my donkey's behaviour too. So I'm washing her ears as well.'

And so, Lao Tzu's disciples understood the importance of not hearing or saying negative words.

At the age of 160, Lao Tzu left his people and went far away to meditate and lead a peaceful life in his final years.

He left in a wooden chariot drawn by a black bull. He rode for a long time till he came to the Han Ku Pass in the north-western frontier of China. The guardian of the pass was a man named Yin Tsi, an ardent devotee of Lao Tzu.

'How can you leave without leaving us a legacy?' Yin Tsi pleaded.

'What can I give you?' asked Lao Tzu. 'My donkey is dead. I have this bull now. Do you want it?'

'What can we do with a bull? What we want is a message, explaining to us how to lead a good life on earth and find our way to heaven,' replied Yin Tsi. 'Please write a book for the good of mankind. This is the debt you have to pay to the world.'

Lao Tzu was touched by his sincere request. He sat at Han Ku Pass for three days and wrote a book called *Tao Te Ching*. Yin Tsi humbly took charge of it and promised to pass it on to the world.

Lao Tzu departed from that place, and Yin Tsi watched in wonderment as the master went drifting through Central Asia and Tibet, his silvery white hair flying in the air and lighting up the skies. Finally, a white stork came down and carried him away to heaven. The clouds chanted his message of kindness, tolerance and peace.

Lao Tzu's disciples did not weep because he was gone. Instead, they assembled and remembered in silence what he had taught them.

The message of the *Tao Te Ching* spread throughout China and farther. Its 81 verses essentially taught the way of living in the world in peace and harmony.

But how could the *Tao Te Ching*, with its five thousand Chinese characters, be read and understood by the rest of the world, wondered Yin Tsi.

And so, over the years, translators made the book accessible to everyone, and Taoist teachers explained it. The message of *Tao Te Ching* came to be known to all.

***

A lightning peek into the Tao Te Ching:

The Way of Heaven is like a well, which is properly used but never used up.

To know others is intelligence; knowing yourself is wisdom.

To conquer others is power; to conquer yourself is strength.

To be content with yourself is to be rich; to be discontent with yourself is to be poor.

To know that you don't know is wise; to think you know when you don't know is not.

What is the gentlest of all overcomes the hardest of all.

He whose braveness lies in war kills.

He whose braveness lies in peace gives life.

True words are not always fine-sounding; fine-sounding words are not always true.

The wise one has few things, but he gives them away and look! He has even more than before.

THE GREATEST WONDER

Yudhishthira lost the game of dice he played with his cousin Duryodhana. He had pawned everything he possessed in the game and now had practically nothing to call his own. Duryodhana banished him and his brothers, the other Pandavas, Bheema, Arjuna, Nakula and Sahadeva, from the kingdom. They had to live in the forest for 12 long years.

'Life in the forest is going to be so agonizing! What will we do under the trees day in and day out?' Bheema and Arjuna moaned. Nakula and Sahadeva woefully nodded along.

Yudhishthira consoled them and said, 'Let us live a life of dharma, wherever we are. It will stand us in good stead...'

'You're forever talking of dharma,' Bheema said angrily. 'Dharma didn't really help when you were playing dice, did it?'

Yudhishthira chose to keep quiet.

But contrary to their expectations, life in their ashram in the forest turned out to be interesting. No two days were the same. The brothers learnt to appreciate the beautiful colours of dawn, the splash of hues of dusk, the myriad sounds of the forest and the company of trees. Despite the hardships of forest life, they began to like their time there.

One morning, an elderly sage rushed into their ashram, looking greatly agitated. 'I have lost my churning staff and iron rods, without which I cannot perform my daily rites. An enormous deer with antlers like the spreading branches of a tree ran towards me. In a split second, the staff and rods stuck to its horns and it turned and ran away. Please help me get my things back,' said the sage, all in one breath.

Yudhishthira was only too ready to help.

'It is our dharma to help the holy man,' he said to his brothers. Bheema opened his mouth to say something, but Nakula stopped him. All of them followed Yudhishthira quietly as he hastened into the depths of the forest in search of the deer, following its hoof marks. After some distance there were no more prints, and they searched for the deer all day long.

It was almost sunset when Sahadeva finally happened to spot the deer. Arjuna sprang forward, and shot an arrow at it. But the deer was too quick for him. It dodged the arrow and vanished from sight.

Overcome by fatigue, the brothers dropped to the ground under a tree. Yudhishthira asked Nakula, the most skilled among them at climbing trees, to climb up and look for any sign of water nearby.

In a few moments, Nakula called out from the topmost branch of the tree, 'I can see some green patches quite close by.' He quickly came down and hastened in that direction. Sure enough, he found a pond of clean water there. He fell down to his knees, splashed the water on his face and was about to drink when he heard a loud voice:

'Stop! The pool is mine. You cannot drink the water till you've answered my questions.'

Nakula hesitated and looked around, but found no one. Thirst drove him to drink the water in spite of the command.

The next moment, he fell down dead.

When there was no sign of Nakula for a long time, the others started getting anxious.

'Where has our eldest brother's guiding spirit of dharma taken Nakula?' Bheema muttered under his breath.

Yudhishthira sent Sahadeva to find out. Sahadeva, too, suffered the same fate as Nakula when he took a sip of the forbidden water. Arjuna and Bheema soon followed suit.

Left alone, Yudhishthira proceeded to the lake. In the eerie silence and gathering darkness, when he saw the dead bodies of his brothers, he was beside himself with shock and grief. He immediately stepped into the water and cleansed himself to perform the last rites for his dear brothers. At the same time, the resonating voice rang out loud and clear, 'Don't be rash like your brothers. First answer my questions and then use the water. Otherwise, you die like them.'

'Whoever you are, I'll obey you, but please tell me why it is a fatal crime to quench one's thirst.' The humility in Yudhishthira's voice and his readiness to uphold his dharma to obey was overwhelming. All of a sudden, an immense, dazzling figure, towering over the surroundings, materialized from the lake. Its voice reiterated the command without answering Yudhishthira's question.

Nevertheless, the Pandava stood with his hands folded, ready to answer the questions of the radiant personality.

'What makes the sun rise? What causes it to set?' was the first question.

Yudhishthira answered, 'By virtue of the dharma or the inherent nature of the creator Brahma, the sun rises and sets.'

More questions followed in quick succession. They were profound and significant, but at times a little mysterious and confusing. They jumped from one topic to another, and there was no time to think. Yudhishthira forgot to breathe. He had to be alert and focused – there was no room for confusion. He had to be clear in his mind. The answers had to be precise and immediate.

'What is important for those who sow?'

'Rain.'

'What is faster than the wind?'

'The mind.'

'What sleeps with its eyes open?'

'A fish.'

'What remains immobile even after being born?'

'An egg.'

'What is one's highest duty?'

'To be non-violent.'

'What is mercy? '

'Showing kindness to all creatures.'

'What is wickedness?'

'Speaking ill of and wishing ill for others.'

'What is harder than steel?'

'The unity between people who love one another.'

'What is as large as the sea?'

'A virtuous woman's heart.'

The questions seemed endless. They came cascading ruthlessly. They touched upon difficult topics like renunciation, surrender, freedom and liberation. Yudhishthira was now faint with thirst.

At long last came the final question. It was a tricky one.

'What is the greatest wonder?'

Yudhishthira thought for a moment.

'Hmm...are you stumped?' the voice said sneeringly.

Yudhishthira did not give up. He replied, 'Every day, we see death. But people never realize that they

will also die one day. They talk and plan as though they will live forever. This is the greatest wonder of the world.' A hush fell for a moment. Then, all of a sudden, Yudhishthira's brothers, who lay lifeless beside him, got up as though from deep slumber. Yudhishthira stood awestruck.

The ordeal was over.

The radiant figure finally revealed himself to the eldest Pandava. It was Yama*, the god of death, Yudhishthira's divine father. He addressed Yudhishthira, 'You have pleased me, my son, with your humility, intelligence and righteousness. These qualities will protect you and your brothers for the rest of your lives.'

Dharma, a significant and oft-used word in Hindu scripture, essentially means righteousness or uprightness.

*Yama was also known as Dharmaraja, the 'king of justice'.

THE MIRACLE WORKER

Jesus was in a thoughtful mood. He was feeling a little confused. How would he teach the people of his land to live in unity? There was violence and strife all around. People only knew how to be angry with each other, and they turned a deaf ear to whatever Jesus had to say and criticized him harshly.

There was one way, Jesus thought, brightening up. He had the power to perform miracles, which would attract people to him, bring them closer, and then he would gradually create a new faith in them. His teachings would then bear fruit and make them live as decent human beings should.

One day, Jesus and his mother, Mary, were invited to the wedding feast of a dear friend. The wine was heavenly and the food delicious. There were many people at the feast. As more arrived, the host was dismayed to find that he was running out of wine. How could there be a wedding feast without wine? Pale-faced with embarrassment, the host did not know where to look. Mary noticed this and whispered into Jesus's ears, 'You have to do something!'

Jesus asked the waiters to fill six jars up to the brim with water.

'Why water?' the waiters wondered. 'We need to serve wine, not water!'

Nevertheless, they obeyed. Next, Jesus asked them to fill the guests' empty wine cups.

'Fill wine cups with water? This is ridiculous!' thought the host. But there was nothing he could do.

As the servers filled the cups, it was not water that flowed but wine. The host and the waiters were dumbstruck. The guests enjoyed the wine more than before. And the news of the water that turned magically into wine spread like wildfire.

'What an amazing miracle! Maybe he has amazing things to say. Perhaps we should listen to him,' the people of the land said to each other with curiosity.

***

The Sea of Galilee lies in the north-east of Israel. Jesus was fond of walking on its shores, watching the azure sky and the horizon merge softly.

One morning, the sea was especially calm, with just a few small waves lapping the shores. Jesus, equally calm, walked slowly, gazing far into the sea. People noticed him and began to gather on the shore, hoping he would say something.

Jesus saw a boat approaching the shore. It looked like a fishing boat. When it was close enough he beckoned to it. The fisherman, whose name was Peter, anchored the boat, and Jesus got into it.

He turned and faced the people, spreading his arms as though welcoming them, and spoke in a gentle voice about how love and humility could win over not just friends but also enemies. The crowd listened quietly. This was something completely new to them! A few people nodded. Many others shook their heads with a doubtful frown. Jesus smiled to himself. He knew it would take time for people to understand. But at least a beginning had been made.

The crowd began to disperse slowly. Many walked away. A few lingered, wondering if he had anything more to say. Jesus said nothing more. He simply asked Peter to sail into deeper waters. Peter wondered why, but he obeyed. When the boat had sailed ahead a little, Jesus asked Peter and the other fishermen in the boat to cast their net into the sea to catch fish. This made no sense to Peter. The men had been fishing all night and had not caught a single fish. Moreover, fishing was done only at night. At daybreak, when the sky lights up, the fish swim deeper into the waters, making it almost impossible to catch them. Nevertheless, the men obeyed without a word. The net was cast out into the sea.

In just a few moments, the net began to feel heavy. The men tugged and tugged, and finally with a lot of effort they pulled it onto the boat. In utter disbelief, they looked at the fish squirming in the net and then they turned to Jesus, who just nodded and smiled.

'Shall we sail back to the shore?' he asked in a gentle voice.

Coming out of his stupor, Peter apologized, in a trembling voice, 'I am sorry I doubted you. In spite of it, you were kind and loving to me.'

Jesus replied softly, 'Don't worry, Peter. Be the same to others and see what wonders it can work.'

It is said that Jesus performed many miracles like these. The Gospel of John, in the Bible, talks about seven of these important miracles. These acts showed his immense love for people and the ways in which he helped them when they needed him most.

THE PROPHET AND HIS DEVOTEES

Prophet Muhammad is revered and honoured by all those who follow Islam. He is the gentle voice on earth of the all-knowing, all powerful, all-pervading God, Allah.

One day, overwhelmed by their dedication, the Prophet said to his devotees compassionately, 'I would like to give you something. Tell me – what can I offer you?'

'You have already given us your wonderful teachings. What more is there for us to ask?' they said.

But one young fellow said something different. He told the Prophet, 'Please give me some time to think. I don't wish to waste this golden opportunity.'

The Prophet smiled kindly and said, 'There is no hurry. You may take your time.'

The very next day, the boy made his request. 'Please tell Allah to make me your neighbour in heaven.'

The Prophet was amazed to hear this unusual request. The others were amused.

'How did you think of such an extraordinary wish?' the Prophet asked.

The boy laughed and said, 'First of all, this wish, if granted, assures me of a special place in heaven.'

He continued, 'Nothing in this world is permanent. Neither money nor happiness will last for eternity. Why should I ask for temporary things? So I decided to ask for something that can last forever.'

The Prophet patted the boy's shoulders and said, 'So shall it be, Inshaallah!'

He then looked at all his devotees and said, 'Being devoted and pious and leading the life of a good Muslim will please Allah greatly. At the same time, remember to pay special attention to prayer. That is the most powerful key to open the golden gates to heaven.'

A few days later, Prophet Muhammad said to his devotees, 'Today, I want you to pay attention to three questions I will ask you. Try to answer them honestly.'

The devotees were all ears. The Prophet said:

'Number one, which one of you stays up all night to pray?

'Number two, who recites the Quran in its entirety every day?

'Number three, which of you fasts every day of the month?'

The devotees were aghast. There was pin-drop silence among them. Some of them looked at one another questioningly, others looked at their palms for inspiration, while some others bit their lips and dug their toenails into the carpet beneath their feet. No one could answer the Prophet's strange questions.

After a few still moments, a high-pitched voice broke the silence. The same young boy from the day before answered. He simply said, 'I do.'

Everyone looked at him in utter disbelief. There were mutterings and mumblings. 'Impossible. He is out of his mind. He's a trickster. He's only trying to please the master!'

'How do you do that?' the Prophet asked the boy. He did not disbelieve him and was eager to hear more.

With great humility, the boy said, 'You have taught us, great master, that cleansing oneself before going to bed is like worshipping Allah all night. I never forget to clean my body every night and I also spend a few minutes getting rid of unwanted thoughts from my mind. I consider this to be like staying up all night and worshipping Allah.'

The other devotees frowned upon hearing these words. Some of them put up their hands as though they wanted to say something. The Prophet shook his head and quietened them.

The boy continued, 'You have also taught us, dear master, the special verse in the Quran, which, when read, is equivalent to reading the entire Quran. So I read this verse three times a day, without fail.

'Thirdly, I fast three days in a month.'

One of the devotees got up and protested, 'That does not at all answer the master's third question.' Again, the Prophet quietened them.

The boy explained further, 'Allah says in the Quran that if you do one good deed, He showers you with ten times that goodness. So, if I fast three times, it is like fasting for a whole month.' The boy stopped and bowed deeply. 'Please correct me if I am wrong.'

'Well done,' said Prophet Muhammad, looking pleased. 'Your answers show that you have paid attention to my words as well as those in the Quran and that you are putting into practice whatever has been taught to you.'

Prophet Muhammad was a great teacher. His students were not just passive listeners. He made them think and encouraged them to ask questions. He, in turn, asked them thought-provoking questions.

THE FOUR SIGHTS

Siddhartha, the crown prince of the kingdom of Sakhya, was a broad-chested, handsome youth. Equally charming and beautiful was his dainty wife, Yashodhara. Deeply in love with each other, they enjoyed their married life in the luxury of the royal home of Maharaja Sudhodana.

They loved walking around the palace gardens, which were profusely sprinkled with green lawns, blooming flowers of every hue and trees with honey-sweet fruits of every variety.

One bright morning in the lovely spring season, Yashodhara spied an irresistibly pretty rose of an unusual hue smiling at her. She extended her hand as though to pluck it. Siddhartha jumped.

'No, Yasho! Don't do that,' he cried. Yashodhara was taken aback. Her hand fell and she looked at her husband, aghast.

'I'm sorry, Yasho,' he said in a milder tone. 'It's just that I thought the flower may feel hurt if it is plucked.'

The couple walked in silence till they reached the outer edge of the garden. Siddhartha and Yashodhara were forbidden to go any further. Yashodhara had lived outside the palace before their wedding, but Siddhartha had so far seen nothing beyond the boundaries of the palace.

Today, both of them were tempted to go out. The guards were not at the gate.

'Perhaps they have gone to watch the fields being readied for sowing. This is our chance. Let's go,' said Yashodhara excitedly. Siddhartha was equally excited, if not more. Hand in hand, they ran out of the palace gates.

Out in the open, they soon saw farmers tilling their fields. It was a breathtaking sight for Siddhartha. Hiding from view, he watched the closest farmer intently. The plough cut the earth, the buffaloes pulled the plough and the farmer drove the animals in rhythmic monotony. It was an everyday sight for the villagers but Siddhartha watched with awe and wonder.

After some time, the farmer slowed down, dripping with sweat and breathing heavily. The tired buffaloes stopped moving. Out came the farmer's whip. *CRACK* it went ruthlessly against the thick hide of the animals. Siddhartha winced and gripped Yashodhara's arm.

The buffaloes refused to budge. The farmer gave up. He released the buffaloes, left the plough for the morrow and turned to go home. For a moment Siddhartha's gaze met the farmer's. Siddhartha loosened his grip on his wife, closed his eyes and slumped to the ground. For a long moment, he sat still. Yashodhara stared at him nervously. When he opened his eyes, she asked with concern, 'What happened? Is anything wrong?'

'It's…it's just something that I've never felt before.' Too perplexed to say anything, Yashodhara waited anxiously for him to continue.

Siddhartha said, 'That farmer is like me…and I'm like him. I felt like…he was my brother…'

He took a breath and continued, 'Peasants are different from royals; they are lesser mortals. This is what we have been taught, right? But now, I realize that they are not different from us. They breathe just like us. Their skin is darkened by the sun and their hands roughened by the hard work they do. These are but external differences. Their hearts beat like yours or mine. The buffaloes? What suffering they go through! Such heavy animals being pulled by a nose ring!'

Yashodhara shivered at Siddhartha's words. They expressed his agony.

'It's getting late. We should be getting back home before they start missing us,' she said gently.

The two of them returned in silence.

The sun set and the sun rose. The world went on as usual. Siddhartha continued to be a loving husband. At the same time, now and then, his thoughts carried him to a different world, raising a thousand questions in his mind.

As time went by, Siddhartha's desire to see more of the outside world increased steadily. He ran to the stables one day and asked the charioteer to take him out. The charioteer froze. 'My head will roll down if I do that, dear prince,' he said in a trembling voice.

'My father is away on a goodwill mission to neighbouring places with his ministers. The guards are playing truant. We will not be missed. Come on!' Siddhartha persisted.

The charioteer could not refuse the young prince's request.

The chariot tore through the air and sped down the serpentine path outside the palace gates. Siddhartha sat mesmerized. He wanted to go on and on. But after a while the horses were tired. They slowed down, and the chariot stopped near a stream. The horses drank water and grazed nearby. Both the men stretched to rest.

Suddenly, Siddhartha sat up. What met his eyes was something he'd never seen before. He watched wide-eyed as an old man, bent double, plodded along the riverside with a crumbling stick in hand for support. Siddhartha was terror-stricken.

'What is that, charioteer?' he asked in a low voice.

'Nothing unusual, Your Highness. Just an old man.'

'Does everyone become old and infirm? You and I included?' asked Siddharth in utter disbelief. The charioteer looked down at his feet and nodded. The young prince watched in dismay as the old man slowly walked away.

Sapped of all enthusiasm, Siddhartha got up to leave. He sat in the chariot with his eyes closed, lost in his thoughts. He was only shaken out of his reverie when the chariot jolted as it encountered rough terrain.

'Stop!' he cried. 'Charioteer, what do I see here under the tree?'

The charioteer saw a man afflicted with a skin disease. Blood oozed from boils that covered his limbs.

Siddhartha was terribly shaken.

'He's diseased, dear prince. Let's not tarry here,' the charioteer said gently.

'Is he in pain?'

'Yes,' the charioteer nodded, avoiding Siddhartha's eyes, slowly increasing the speed of the chariot. The prince sat back, stunned and speechless.

The chariot moved ahead fast now. Siddhartha had been out for too long, and the charioteer was really worried.

Suddenly the chariot had to brake. A group of men, dressed in white, were crossing the road slowly, chanting mournfully. They were followed by four others carrying a wooden stretcher on their shoulders. A few more men followed the stretcher.

Before Siddhartha could ask anything, the charioteer volunteered, 'That's a funeral procession, Your Highness. The person on the stretcher is dead.'

'Dead? Does everybody die, charioteer? You and I too?'

'Yes. Death happens to everybody sooner or later,' said the charioteer quietly.

The procession was gone, and the chariot drove homewards. The chanting of the mourners kept ringing in Siddhartha's ears.

That night, Siddhartha lay wide awake in bed. His thoughts were in utter turmoil. The scenes he had witnessed that day flashed before his mind's eye repeatedly. Why was there so much pain and suffering, sickness and sorrow in the world? Hasn't life anything better to offer? Answers had to be found.

A change had begun in Siddhartha's inner being. It made him realize that he could no longer be the same loving husband, respectful son and majestic crown prince that he had been all this time. He would have to go in search of something more profound in life, beyond joy, sorrow, pain, suffering and unreasonable religious and social norms.

Siddhartha lingered in the palace for a while longer, though his mind was elsewhere. Yashodhara was shocked by the change that had come over him. His parents were also disturbed. The last smile that lit up his face was when Yashodhara told him that she was going to deliver his child in a few weeks. But that did not stop him from going away. Soon, the palace bid Siddhartha goodbye.

He would return later as the Buddha to spread his message of universal brotherhood and purposeful living.

Why was Prince Siddhartha barred from leaving the boundaries of the palace? When he was born, his father, King Sudhodana, was told by a group of sages that Siddhartha would grow up to be either a great king or a monk. The king was intent on his son taking over his throne. He knew that if Siddhartha saw the harsh realities of life, he would turn to a different path, which is why he kept him in the midst of luxury and refused to let him see the outside world.

THE 14TH DALAI LAMA

His Holiness the 14th Dalai Lama calls himself a simple Buddhist monk. He lives in Dharamshala, a town in the Himalayan foothills of India.

He is said to have been born with his eyes wide open. Everyone was awestruck, and wise men predicted that the child's life would be spiritually oriented. True to their prediction, he became the one to take on the mantle from the 13th Dalai Lama as the spiritual leader of the Tibetan people.

As the future leader, his life was confined to a Tibetan Buddhist monastery meant to groom monks from the tender age of six. He began learning the basic principles of Buddhism and several other related subjects. His daily routine was a strict one, filled with prayers, chanting, meditation and studies. Meals were frugal and sleep, minimal. He had no chance to contact the outside world. And yet, he was not only an excellent student but he also had other interests. In his teens, his fondness and natural aptitude for machines became well known. This was proved when he fixed a movie projector in the monastery without any instructions or a guide book. If he had not become a spiritual leader, he would have been a good engineer! Finally, after years of rigorous study, he got a doctorate in Buddhist philosophy.

The Dalai Lama is a man of peace. But life did not let him remain in peace. When Chinese soldiers trooped into Tibet to make it part of China, his devotees, who loved and respected him greatly, were keen to protect him. Although he was reluctant to leave his fellow Tibetans in danger, they packed him off in the dead of night, in disguise, through a less known path to India. He was given asylum by the Indian government, and he made Dharamshala his home.

He consistently talked of peace and tried to persuade Chinese political leaders to free Tibet. He was awarded the Nobel Peace Prize for his non-violent struggle for the liberation of Tibet.

'What are you doing with your anger, pride and jealousy?' he says. 'Throw them away to the four winds and purify yourselves. Be compassionate. That is the source of our well-being. Paying regard to religion is optional, but disregarding the quality of compassion is a mistake.'

'What is compassion?' people ask him.

'Being warm-hearted towards one and all. That is enough. It works like magic to understand the oneness of humanity and to create a happier and more peaceful world.'

The Dalai Lama continues to live in Dharamshala and preaches not only to Tibetans but to all of India and the rest of the world. He is a world leader today, spreading the message of peace and unity.

But he's not a serious man! 'Laughing is one of my favourite things,' he confesses. In spite of all the hardships he has had to face in life, his ready smile, great sense of humour and child-like attitude have remained intact.

BLACK BEAUTY

The Buddha sat under the vast tree, cross-legged, eyes half-closed, palms upturned on his thighs. His chest moved up and down slowly as he breathed. Not a leaf stirred. Not a bird chirped. The disciples surrounding him sat in silence, trying to be as composed as he was. They waited to hear him speak.

The senior disciples whispered, 'Our guru is compassion personified.' The others nodded but they were not quite sure what compassion meant. They wanted the Buddha to tell them about it.

The Buddha cleared his throat and began to speak. 'There once lived a rich farmer. Acres of green farms surrounded his sprawling home. The rains were good and the harvest was plentiful year after year. Wealth and good health kept the household happy. Even the animals in the farmyard were content!

'One day, everyone was particularly happy. One of the cows had given birth to a black bull calf. When the farmer saw how strong and perfectly formed the calf was, he stroked him gently and whispered in his ear, "You are my Black Beauty." The young bull became a favourite of the farmer and was fed the finest food on the farm.

'Black Beauty grew up to be a giant bull with amazing strength. He nodded gratefully whenever the farmer fondly stroked and patted him. He felt deeply indebted to his master and he thought, "I must repay my master's kindness. But how?" For a long time he thought about this. At last, he came up with a solution. He told the farmer to hold a contest for bulls from all the neighbouring farms.

'"What sort of contest?" asked the farmer.

'"A prize of a thousand gold coins for the bull that can pull a cartload of stones to the finishing line first."

'The farmer liked the bull's idea. He was sure none would stand a chance against Black Beauty. The losers would have to pay a thousand gold coins each to Black Beauty. What a windfall that would be, thought the farmer. Gold coins dazzled in his mind's eye.

'The contest was announced and all the farmers began to prepare their bulls for the tournament. The bulls had a tough time practising pulling carts loaded with stones several times a day.

'The day of the contest dawned bright and beautiful. The bulls were ready with their carts.

'At the stroke of the gong, the farmers drove their bulls ahead. The spectators screamed in delight.

'The bulls moved slowly. The load was far too heavy for them to move faster. Even Black Beauty, with all his strength, moved slowly.

'Suddenly, Black Beauty felt the lightning stroke of the farmer's whip on his back. He was stunned. He had never been whipped before. Again, another fierce stroke of the whip landed. Black Beauty slowed down.

'Once again, the farmer whipped him and yelled furiously, "Pull…pull, you demon!" Black Beauty froze. He did not budge another inch. The whip landed again and again. But Black Beauty did not move, and the other bulls soon overtook him. The race was over. Black Beauty had lost.

'Back at the farm, Black Beauty faced the disappointed farmer with a tear-stained face and asked him softly, "You have never laid a hand on me in all these years. You've never spoken a harsh word to me. Yet you whipped me with such unbelievable ferocity today, though I pulled as well as I could. Why?"

'The farmer realized his mistake. It was the thought of gold that had made him such a monster. He was ashamed. He thought, "What if Black Beauty had lost his temper, thrown me down and trampled me? Even a bull is more compassionate than me!"

'The farmer tended to Black Beauty's wounds and fed him with his own hands. It took several days for Black Beauty to regain his strength.

'Much to Black Beauty's surprise, the farmer announced another contest. The prize was two thousand gold coins. This time, Black Beauty won.'

Buddhist stories known as the Jataka Tales celebrate the power of compassion, love, wisdom, kindness and all the other values upheld and preached by the Buddha.

The Buddha told many such stories to his disciples more than two thousand years ago. About five hundred of them have survived and have been translated into several languages the world over.

THE MYSTICAL CART DRIVER

There once lived a king who was greatly loved by his subjects, and rightly so. He was kind and generous, and would never turn away anyone in need. Every day, extra food was prepared in the palace kitchens, which would be distributed among the poor so no one ever went hungry in the kingdom.

The towns and villages were well maintained. They were beautified with fountains, lotus ponds and gardens. There were comfortable rest houses for travellers. Flora and fauna thrived in the forest areas.

The ministers respected their king and willingly obeyed his commands.

'I have gained a special place in the hearts of my people. I'm sure God will bestow me with his blessings for all that I'm doing for them,' the king would often say to himself.

One evening, as usual, he was sitting on his silken couch in the balcony of his royal chambers. He took a deep breath. The scent of the orchids that lined the balcony was soothing. He let out a sigh of satisfaction. Sipping his cup of warm milk flavoured with saffron, he watched the sun hugging the western horizon. The sky was ablaze with pink and orange. Silhouetted against the colourful sky, a couple of geese flew gracefully past the palace. The king, who knew the language of the birds, heard them talking to each other.

'Take care not to fly over the king's balcony,' the first goose warned the second.

'Why?' the second one asked.

'How ignorant are you? Don't you know that a radiant aura of greatness surrounds the king? So brilliant is the aura that if you fly too close, you might get burnt by it.'

The second goose honked in contempt and said, 'Anyone would think you are talking about Raikva and not the king.'

'Who's that?'

'Don't you know about the one with the cart…' The geese flew away out of hearing, leaving the king wondering about this Raikva. He sat, lost in deep thought, till a million stars twinkled in the dark sky and a gibbous moon shed its pale light on him.

The king tossed and turned in his bed all night and fell into a slumber only in the early hours of the morning. He woke up a worried man, his thoughts still full of 'Raikva'.

He sent for one of his soldiers. 'Did you hear somebody talk about Raikva last night?' he asked.

The soldier shook his head in puzzlement.

'Go then and look for Raikva with the cart, and come back with a report!'

The bewildered soldier set out to carry out the king's orders, not knowing who Raikva was and where to look for him.

The soldier spent the whole day going door to door asking for Raikva.

He got no answer. Finally he had to go back to the king reporting failure.

'Search again!' said the annoyed king. 'Look in the market or on the riverbanks or the woods – look everywhere! Make sure you cover every inch of the kingdom.'

The obedient soldier went on another search expedition. This time, he was successful. He found Raikva in a quiet corner of the marketplace. To protect himself from the blazing sun, he was lying under his cart. The soldier looked at him. He was dressed in ordinary, nondescript clothes. Yet, a special aura surrounded him. The soldier went closer. He suddenly felt inexplicably joyous.

He asked the man under the cart, 'Excuse me, but are you Raikva?'

'Indeed I am,' replied the man with a friendly smile. His voice was gentle and soothing. The soldier wanted to stay and talk to him some more, but he had to go back and report to the king.

The king was delighted as well as amazed to hear the soldier's report. He could not wait to meet this unusual person.

Armed with cartloads of riches and goodies, the king set out in his golden chariot with the soldier leading the way. People stared in astonishment at the procession, then burst into cheers and applause when they spotted him.

Finally, the chariot stopped close to Raikva's cart. The king stepped out, and Raikva sat up, looking curiously at him.

The king said, 'I wish to bestow these gifts upon you. No one in my kingdom lives in want.'

The king was sure that Raikva would be excited and overwhelmed by his gifts.

But the cart driver did not even look at them.

He simply said, 'I have no wants. I do not need these gifts. Please take them away.'

The king was shocked.

For a few moments, he just stared at Raikva. In spite of his ordinariness, there was something special about him.

Raikva did not say anything else.

The bewildered king got into his chariot and returned to the palace. The cartloads of gifts went back with him. For the rest of the day, he remained pensive. The encounter with Raikva had been a truly staggering experience for him. The man's peaceful countenance danced in front of his eyes and his gentle voice rang in his ears.

His inner voice spoke to him. 'All that you have means nothing to Raikva. But what he possesses is a treasure that means a lot to *you*.'

The king was awestruck. Several questions tumbled in his mind. 'What is the special treasure that Raikva possesses? Could it be more valuable than all my treasures put together? Will he tell me about it?'

The king longed to meet Raikva again. He was eager to know more about him.

Early the next morning, he got into his chariot and left. Once again, he carried gifts for Raikva, but this time, he presented them to him with humility.

'Please accept my gifts,' he told Raikva. 'What I wish with all my heart is for you to accept me as a student and tell me about the treasure of true peace and happiness that you possess.'

Raikva accepted the gifts with a smile. He realized that the unnecessary pride in the king's mind was gone; humility would enable him to understand. Raikva then began to tell the king how to attain peace of mind and what the scriptures described as true happiness. All this was very different from the lessons the king had ever learnt. He came to Raikva several times to learn more, and each time he went back to the palace deep in thought.

Raikva gave a last piece of advice to the king.

'It is good to be charitable. Give what you can to your people and help them. But remember, the things you give away are not actually yours. They are gifts from nature. Give them in humility. It will make you and them truly happy.'

A great change came over the king. He felt more peaceful than ever before. He carried on with his royal duties without becoming upset or worried. He became a better person who found fulfilment in himself. Besides giving material gifts to his subjects, he was able to give them joy as well. The kingdom was a heavenly place to live in.

The story of Raikva the cart driver comes from the Chandogya Upanishad. The Upanishads are ancient Sanskrit texts that are important in Hinduism.

THE BODY POLITICS

The Persians were peace-loving people. But their leaders, the so-called religious heads, were always at loggerheads with each other over their varying beliefs. There was unrest in the country because of their non-cooperative attitude.

The people grumbled, 'What is the use of living if we cannot live in peace?'

One voice rose loudly and said:

'Inhale the fragrance of fellowship,
Believe in the bondage of brotherhood
And light the lamp of love.'

Curious eyes turned to the voice. It was a tall, middle-aged man who had spoken up. At first, the people were silent, but soon enough, voices erupted in protest and said, 'Mere words, pleasing to the ear. But the idea won't work.'

'Why not? It should, when we learn to accept the earth as one country and all of mankind as its citizens. All religions are but different paths leading to the same godhead,' the tall man persisted boldly. He had been thinking deeply about the welfare of society, and he spoke with conviction. He was known as Baha'ull'ah.

'When there is strife and persecution all around, your speech will only fall on deaf ears,' the people said heatedly.

Baha'u'llah was not one to give up. He talked about equality. He laid down the principles for building a global civilization with one universal religious doctrine that would be acceptable by all.

He had a following, but they were not people who trusted him. They were a critical group who wanted to listen to him and pick faults with his point of view.

The better way to convince anyone about peace and unity would be to tell them a story related to these concepts, Baha'u'llah told himself, and the story would have to be about something everybody was familiar with. He turned to face the people and addressed them in a resonating voice.

'Friends and countrymen, listen to this story! Once upon a time, the different parts of the human body began to think about the respective roles they played in the upkeep of the body.'

The listeners became mildly interested.

Baha'u'llah continued, 'First, the hands spoke up. "We work for many hours of the day to prepare the food required by the body. The stomach gets the benefit of it without doing any work and it thinks it's the source of our life."

'The legs lamented, "We carry the body to the market to get all the food. We also help the hands to cook by enabling them to move around. They can't be in one place all the time. Indeed, the stomach does nothing, but it reaps the harvest of our work."

'Next, it was the turn of the eyes. "If we do not lead the way to the market, the hands and legs cannot get there. Moreover, they need us all through the waking hours for doing their work to support the stomach."

'"Think of us," cried the mouth, teeth and tongue together. "We send the food down to the stomach for it to enjoy. If the food happens to be too salty or insipid or stale or too hard to chew, we throw it up. The stomach gets good, tasty food to eat only because of us."

'"Remember that I do all the thinking for the entire process. The stomach gets the fruit of all our labour put together. It has no thinking to do on its own," said the brain woefully.

'Nothing more was said for some time. The silence was followed by arguments and discussions for a long while, all of which led to one final decision – no more feeding the stomach and accepting it as the source of life.

'When the sun rose, the brain stopped thinking, the legs did not move, the eye refused to lead the way, the hands did no cooking and the mouth, teeth and tongue did nothing. It was a day of rest for all of them.

'The sun set and darkness crept in. A splendid moon smiled at the body. But none of the body parts smiled back. All of them were too weak to smile. They felt giddy. By the end of the next day, they did not have an iota of energy left for any kind of movement. The body lay still, faint with hunger.

'The body parts began to realize that the stomach swallowed the fruits of their labour in order to energize them. It was the source of their strength. They realized they had been wrong and began to work with renewed energy. There was no more grumbling.'

Finally, his followers understood what he was trying to say.

Baha'ull'ah strongly believed that the world could have peace and unity if all races, countries and religions came together, if we all felt like we belonged to one family. This belief led to him establishing a new religion, the Baha'i faith, in his home country of Persia. Eventually, this religion of peace spread throughout the world. Today, India has the world's biggest number of Baha'i followers.

DATTATREYA

In Hindu scriptures, Atri Maharishi is hailed as a great sage. His son Dattatreya was also revered and worshipped. He was calm and gentle, friendly and approachable. People loved to be in his company. Dattatreya was compassionate and kind to his followers, but he also liked to be alone and meditate.

He decided to get rid of all his possessions one day so he could spend time alone and be close to nature. He lived on alms and was happy with whatever people gave him to satisfy his hunger. He had no likes or dislikes and no special wants.

Giving Dattatreya alms was considered special because along with the alms, it was said that he took away the giver's sins as well. He digested the sins along with the food, leaving the giver purer than before.

One day, he encountered the king of the land, Yadu. The king noticed the radiant expression of joy on Dattatreya's face and was intrigued. How could a beggar with no possessions and no roof over his head be so happy? He stopped to speak with Dattatreya and humbly asked him, 'What is the source of your cheerful disposition? You are happy with nothing, whereas even though I possess everything I want, I still want more.'

Dattatreya smiled and replied, 'I am happy because of what I am, not because of what I have.'

The king nodded, trying to understand. He asked him another question. 'May I know who your guru is so that I can also be guided by him?'

'I call myself a disciple of nature,' said Dattatreya with the same smile. 'I have gurus all around me and they teach me very valuable lessons.

'When I look at the sea, I am inspired. It is unmoved by the rivers that flow into it. In the same way, humans should be unmoved by the events of the world.

'Water is the embodiment of calm and purity. I should purify my mind and remain peaceful in its purity.

'Air teaches me freedom. The movement of the air makes the atmosphere pure. I too should keep moving without getting attached to a place or its people. Freedom from attachment is the secret of happiness.

'I have learnt patience from the earth. It puts up with all the hurtful things humans do to it and yet does them good by producing plants and trees, and giving them what they need to survive.

'Fire burns bright. A wise person glows with the splendour of knowledge and good deeds.

'And my guru the spider weaves a beautiful web, gets entangled in it and dies. This teaches me not to accumulate worldly possessions and get entangled in them.'

The king asked, 'May I know how many of these gurus you have?'

Dattatreya could not help but laugh at the question. He said, 'My gurus add up to 24 in all.'

The king fell at Dattatreya's feet and said, 'Hail the disciple of 24 gurus!'

King Yadu abandoned his riches and worldly possessions and followed Dattatreya's path, becoming a student of nature.

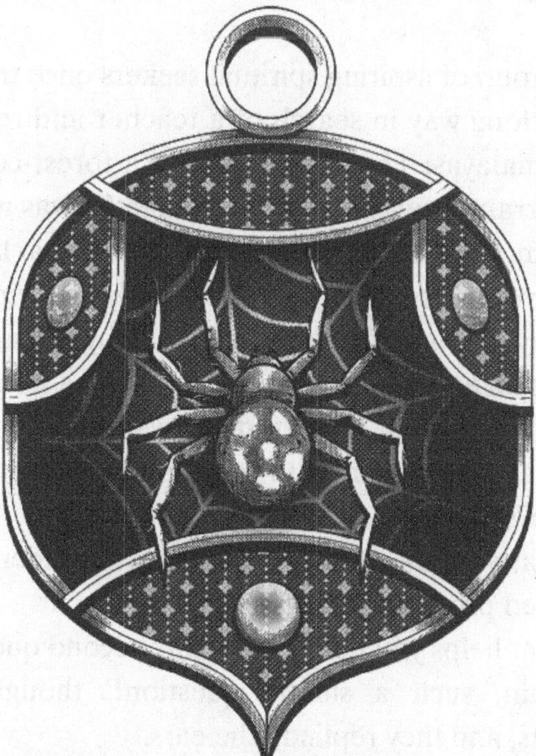

THE MYSTERIOUS FIGURE

A group of aspiring spiritual seekers once trekked a long way in search of a teacher and reached the Himalayas. They found him in a forest-covered hilly terrain. It was almost as though he was waiting for them, and they were delighted. They sat at his feet with reverence. All of them had read the scriptures, but they wanted to know their real significance. It was not an easy task for the teacher. For a long time, he remained silent. The students waited patiently.

At last, he began with a question. 'What helps you see?'

'What an easy question!' thought the students and answered promptly, 'the eyes.'

'What helps you hear?' came the second question.

'Again, such a simple question!' thought the students, and they replied, 'the ears.'

The students fidgeted a bit when the third not-so-simple question came.

'What makes the eye see or the ear hear?' The students looked at each other. They had never thought about what enables the senses to perform their tasks. The teacher then told them about the ultimate superpower, known as the Brahman, that governs the entire universe and all its activities.

'Where can we find this superpower?

'How do we recognize Brahman?'

'How do we pay our respects to this power?'

A volley of questions burst forth.

'Brahman is invisible. It cannot be seen,' was the brief reply.

The students sighed. The teacher continued, 'It is different from whatever you see and interact with in this world. So, it has to be understood and felt in the depths of the heart.'

'This is very difficult to understand,' the students muttered.

'Yes, it is so. That is why this incomprehensible entity reveals itself to us in the form of gods known as devas, who are widely talked about in the sacred texts and worshipped in different ways.'

'Are the devas answerable to Brahman?' a clever student asked.

'Yes. Brahman bestows on them special powers to help the human race and satisfy its needs. They are grateful to it and are aware of its greatness.'

The students nodded silently, trying to grasp whatever they had been told so far.

The teacher was now ready with a story about the devas and their powers. The students sat up eagerly to listen to it. The teacher began.

'The devas were happy with their powers. They used them as and when the need arose. With the passage of time, however, Brahman as the source of their powers was forgotten. The devas thought that they had become powerful of their own accord.

'When Brahman perceived this, it manifested as a mysterious figure and appeared before them. The devas were aghast. They had never ever set eyes on such an awesome figure. It was neither human nor divine. It was neither demonic nor god-like. It did not represent any kind of living being known to them. They stared at it in utter bewilderment. A few moments passed. Then, the fire god stood up and said, "Let me find out who this mysterious figure is and why it has come here."

'Before the fire god could put forth his question, the figure asked him, "Who are you?"

'"I am Agni, the fire god."

'"What power do you possess?"

'"I can burn up whatever comes my way. In fact, I can burn all that exists on earth in the blink of an eye," replied the fire god proudly.

'The figure placed a piece of straw before Agni and asked him to burn it.

'"Is that all?" Agni remarked with a smirk and rushed towards the straw. But he could not burn it. He tried again, but the straw refused to burn.

'Without a word, Agni turned and went back to the devas and confessed his failure. All of them turned to the god of air, Vayu, and requested him to go and find out what was up. Vayu approached the figure as a wild current of air.

'Unperturbed, the figure asked him, "Who are you?"

'"I am Vayu, the god of air."

'"What power do you possess?"

'"I can blow away anything on earth, big or small, heavy or light," replied Vayu, blowing a strong gust of air up into the skies.

'The figure pointed to the straw that Agni could not burn and said, "Blow this away if you can."

'"What makes you think I can't?" Vayu said haughtily and blew the straw as strongly as he could.

'The straw showed no signs of getting blown away. It did not move in the least.

'Vayu returned and told the devas about his unsuccessful mission.

'"I have no clue who this mysterious figure is," he said remorsefully. The devas were greatly disappointed. They now turned with pleading eyes to Indra, the lord of the gods. He set out to solve the mystery with a confident gait. But the moment he reached the figure, it vanished from his sight.

'Indra was taken aback. He stood transfixed, watching the empty space that had been occupied by the figure just a moment ago. Just then, the stunning figure of a beautiful woman, resplendent and bejewelled, appeared before him. He almost swooned when her sweet voice revived him. She explained to him, "What you saw was Brahman. Even a piece of straw is under its command. It is Brahman who has made you powerful. You forgot that you owe your abilities to it, and it came as the mysterious figure to pull you up, and has sent me to remind you of your forgetfulness." Indra hung his head in shame.'

The story interested the students so much that it took them a while to realize that the teacher's voice had trailed off into silence.

The students were eager to learn more about the mysteries of Creation and the Creator. The teacher was pleased with their eagerness and continued to teach them.

When it was finally time for the seekers to go back to their homes, the teacher told them, 'May you spread the knowledge imparted to you to eager seekers who come to you. Never for a moment forget the all-powerful, limitless source of life, Brahman. This will give you the humility, reverence and sense of gratitude needed to lead a good life, untainted by pride or arrogance.'

'We will remember,' chorused the students in one voice.

The tale of the devas is adapted from the Kena Upanishad, one of the most widely interpreted and oft-quoted Upanishads. This text emphasizes that seeking knowledge is the desire of all creatures.

THE 'MAYBE' FARMER

There was once a farmer, a simple man, quiet, hard-working and friendly. The villagers liked and respected him.

He had a son, a young boy, who was a great support on the farm and at home.

The farmer owned a horse, healthy and sturdy, and it was also a great help for him in more ways than one.

The threesome managed their daily living peacefully, whether the weather was wet or dry, hot or cold.

One bright day, things changed. The son called out, 'Father, where's the horse?'

'Must be around somewhere,' replied the farmer, getting out of bed.

'But I've looked everywhere – he's gone!' shouted the son.

The neighbours heard him. In a blink the news spread across the village, and everyone was at the farmer's doorstep.

'Oh, this is too bad! Losing a good working horse is indeed a great misfortune,' they lamented.

When the lamentations died down, the farmer shrugged his shoulders and said, 'Maybe.'

The sun shone and rode the skies as usual and disappeared. The moonlit night was quiet. The farmer slept peacefully, but thc son's slumber was fitful. He dreamed about the horse grazing in heaven.

The next sunrise brought the horse back. He was found grazing near the farm, but he was not alone. He had a beautiful mare with him.

The excited villagers came rushing to the farmer's home. They congratulated him. 'Wow! What a stroke of luck! Two horses in place of one!' they said, expecting the farmer to be delighted.

The farmer just shrugged and said, 'Maybe.'

His reaction left the villagers speechless.

The farmer's son, however, was giddy with joy. He was fascinated by the mare. He wanted to ride her over hill and dale. He asked for his father's permission to buy a saddle.

He brushed the mare well, patted her and put the saddle on. He let the straps down quickly and tightened the tie straps.

The mare stood quietly all this while. But as soon as the boy jumped on her back, she gave a start and began to run at lightning speed.

The boy held on for dear life. But not for long. In just a short while, he was thrown aside wildly, and the mare sped away. The boy rolled down and hit rocky ground. He broke his leg and screamed in pain.

'A bad fracture, my boy,' the doctor said. 'Just bear the pain till I set your leg. No moving your leg after that for the next three weeks.'

The villagers surrounded the boy's bed and sighed heavily. They shook their heads sadly and said, 'Oh, it's too bad. Misfortune has descended in a miserable way.'

They waited to hear what the farmer had to say. But he just shrugged his shoulders and said, 'Maybe.' The villagers were disappointed.

The farmer, in his own quiet way, now looked after the farm, the horse and also the household. He took care of his son's needs too.

A few sunrises later, there was a lot of commotion in the village. Several soldiers on horseback were all over the place. They entered each and every household in search of young men in the families.

'It is time to join the army, every one of you,' they told the young men. 'Our kingdom has been attacked and we need fighters to drive the enemy away. There is no time to waste.' The soldiers made sure that every single youth was taken with them.

Lastly, they entered the farmer's house. They spied the farmer's son in bed and shouted angrily, 'Come on, young man. This is not the time to laze around. Get up and get dressed. Off to the battlefield!' But when they saw his bandaged foot, they were taken aback. They muttered furiously, 'You are of no use to us.' They promptly turned and went away, taking with them the rest of the boys from the village.

The villagers bid their sons a tearful farewell. They kept waving till their dear boys were out of sight. All the other parents were overwhelmed by a pang of jealousy when they saw the farmer.

'Lucky you!' they said bitterly. 'Your son has escaped the horrors of war and is safely at home, while we were forced to give ours away. Who knows if they will return safely or not?' They sighed and said grudgingly, 'Dame Luck has surely smiled on you.'

And they turned and went away without waiting to see the farmer shrug his shoulders and say, 'Maybe.'

This story has its roots in Taoism. It is widely embraced today as a way of life thanks to the teachings of Lao Tzu. With a subtle sense of humour, he liked to tell his followers stories about life that reflected values like simplicity, humility, patience, restfulness and love. He believed that problems get magnified because we worry too much about them. A change of focus and learning to go with the flow can quite often solve the problem.

THE GIVING SUFI

In old Baghdad, there lived a Sufi saint known for his simplicity, melodious voice and sense of humour. He had a following of mostly young people, especially because they could dance ecstatically to his devotional songs. He, in turn, believed that their enthusiasm would lead them eventually to oneness with the almighty.

The saint was of a charitable disposition; he kept giving away his possessions to the needy. He gave away everything he owned, keeping the bare minimum to live a frugal life. But this did not stop him from being charitable. His disciples wondered how their master could give when he had practically nothing to call his own.

Overcome by curiosity, they decided to solve the mystery of their 'giving' master by keeping a 24-hour vigil at his simple abode. And that is how they discovered that he borrowed in order to give away.

'Giving charity on credit? Incredible!' they muttered. But they had to believe it because they saw with their own eyes moneylenders walking into his house and money changing hands.

'How does our master expect to repay his creditors? How do the creditors believe he can repay them?' they thought.

Could it be that his saintly disposition cast them under a divine spell? All sorts of thoughts cascaded in the minds of the bewildered disciples. They felt dizzy and their hearts ached. How could they reprimand their esteemed master or even attempt to reason with him? So they kept quiet.

Suddenly, one day, the saint fell ill. His condition deteriorated rapidly. He refused to eat and became very weak. His failing health became a matter of great concern not only for his disciples but also for his scores of creditors. The people who availed of his charity were sad. The dogs he fed whined in hunger. His home was filled with disciples, creditors and his beneficiaries. They surrounded the bed he lay on. The dogs crouched beneath it. The disciples were distressed and silent. The creditors were annoyed and they grumbled. Their grumbling steadily grew louder, but the saint lay with his eyes closed, quite unmindful of what was happening around him.

After a while, when the disciples could no longer stand the din of the grumbling, they bent low and whispered in the master's ears, 'The creditors are here. They want their money back.'

Without opening his eyes, the saint told them, 'Tell them their money is in God's hands.'

The grumbling grew into an angry buzz.

'Tell them God knows everything,' the master said.

The creditors became even more annoyed, and the disciples became even more disturbed.

All of a sudden, a shrill voice from the roadside rent the air. 'Halwa! *Badam* halwa! *Handi*-fresh badam halwa!'

All the noise immediately came to a stop.

The saint sat up, his face lit up with a smile. He turned to his disciples and inquired in a feeble voice, 'How much for a full plate?'

The disciples found out the price from the shrill-voiced halwa boy and told the saint, 'One silver dirham.'

'No, no. Too much. Only half a silver dirham,' the saint bargained.

The boy protested at first. But one look at the saintly smile on the master's face and he agreed.

A plateful of halwa came to the master's side. Everyone enjoyed a share of the delicious sweet.

They had barely finished licking their fingers when the halwa boy shrieked, 'Where's my money?'

All eyes turned to the saint, questioningly.

The saint, unperturbed, said, 'I lowered the price but did not say that I would pay.'

The poor boy groaned. 'My precious halwa has gone for free!' he wailed. 'I'm ruined!'

There was an uproar from the creditors. 'First we have been cheated and now it's the poor halwa boy. This saintly figure on his deathbed is a trickster of the lowest order,' they shouted. The din became unbearable. The disciples felt hopeless and were horrified. Only the saint sat calm and composed.

Suddenly, a well-dressed messenger walked up to the bedside and handed an envelope to the saint. Eager faces watched the saint tear open the envelope. One silver dirham fell out of it. There was a loud gasp from everyone and then a hush fell. The saint quietly handed the money to the halwa boy, who promptly grabbed it and ran away. The creditors shot daggers at the saint. Before they could do anything else, the messenger appeared again, this time with a packet. The saint opened it carefully. The jingling sound of coins came from it. The saint gave the money to his disciples to count.

'One, two, three...' They counted one hundred silver dirhams. The saint gave the money to his creditors and said, 'Share it among yourselves.'

'But this is only a part of what you owe us,' they cried. The saint just waved them away, lay down and breathed his last.

The creditors left with an audible shower of curses, leaving the disciples to mourn.

After performing the last rites for their master, the disciples sat together to talk about his greatness. But not a word did they utter. They just thought and thought. At last, one of them said, 'Our master is surely a great saint. By his unforgettable deeds, he has reminded us not only about the importance of charity but also how God takes care of us if we surrender totally.'

'What about the halwa boy?'

'What about him? He got his money because he is an honest worker. The creditors known for their dishonesty were partially paid back. They got what they deserved.'

'Our master is truly great,' they said together. In his fond memory, they burst into song and danced ecstatically.

Have you ever seen whirling dervishes? They are Sufis, often seen in Turkey, who wear long robes and dance to music as a form of meditation. Music and dance are very important to them because they think these deepen one's bond with God.

KABIR

Kabir Das was a 15th-century Indian mystic, poet and saint. Varanasi was his home. It is said that he was born to a Hindu family but was picked up as a foundling by a Muslim family of weavers. He too was brought up to be a weaver, and work was worship for Kabir.

From an early age his thoughts were different from others. He contemplated things greater than mundane worldly activities. He was influenced by the Islamic tradition of Sufism. At the same time, he wanted to become a disciple of Swami Ramananda, a Hindu sage. One day, he approached the swami and expressed his wish to be devoted to him. Ramananda, being a devout Hindu, refused to take Kabir as his disciple because the latter was a Muslim weaver. He did not think Kabir would understand Hindu scriptures.

The next morning, when the swami came to the banks of the Ganga to bathe, he found Kabir sitting there, eyes shut, softly uttering the name of Ram. The swami looked at him in wonder. His heart told him that he would be making a grave mistake if he did not take Kabir as his disciple. He started teaching Kabir the same day.

Kabir brought Islam and Hinduism under one roof and preached the concept of one true God who ruled all of Creation. Therefore, there should be no difference between a Muslim and a Hindu. Ram and Allah are just different names given to the same supreme being. Moreover, all men and women were seen by Kabir as living forms of God. Hindus and Muslims were equally inspired by Kabir. Sikh religious leaders, too, agreed with his views and included his sayings in their scripture, the Guru Granth Sahib.

When Kabir passed away, both Hindus and Muslims claimed him as theirs and wanted to perform the last rites according to their respective traditions. The Hindus wanted to cremate him, and the Muslims wished to bury him. While this argument went on, someone lifted the cloth that covered Kabir's dead body. In place of the body was a heap of flowers!

Kabir is considered to be a teacher of a universal religion. He often said, 'Be good, do good and be devoted to God in whatever form you worship Him.' His sayings are called *doha*s. People loved the sing-song rhythm of the *doha*s and would sing along with him. Later on they were written out by his devotees and passed down to future generations.

Sant Kabir Das Math, which was built in his memory in Varanasi, is a place of peace. Saints from all over the world visit the *math*, sing *doha*s to their hearts' content and go back inspired.

***

Who can turn away from Kabir's *doha*s?

'Love is not grown on trees or bought in the market; if one wants to be loved one must know how to give love.'

'If you want the truth, I'll tell you the truth. Just listen to the secret sound, the real sound which echoes within you.'

Several of his *dohas* boldly question the misplaced beliefs and rituals of his time.

'If God is inside the mosque,
Then to whom does the world belong?
If Rama is within an image,
Then who is there to know what happens without?
Look within your heart and you will find both Rahim and Rama.
If there is a simple way to go to heaven, just by dying in Kasi,
Then what is the necessity of worshipping God?'